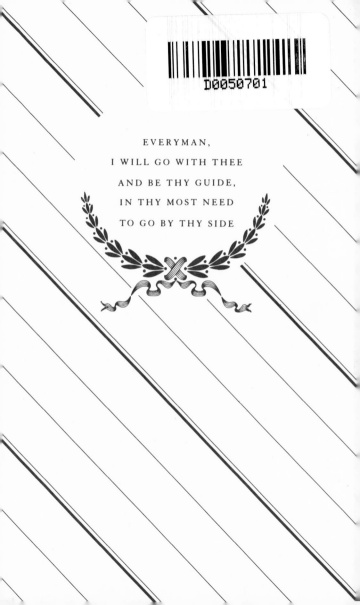

EVERYMAN,
I WILL GO WITH THEE
AND BE THY GUIDE,
IN THY MOST NEED
TO GO BY THY SIDE

EVERYMAN'S LIBRARY
POCKET POETS

MOTHERHOOD

POEMS ABOUT MOTHERS

SELECTED AND EDITED BY
CARMELA CIURARU

EVERYMAN'S LIBRARY
POCKET POETS

Alfred A. Knopf New York London Toronto

THIS IS A BORZOI BOOK
PUBLISHED BY ALFRED A. KNOPF

This selection by Carmela Ciuraru first published in
Everyman's Library, 2005
Copyright © 2005 by Everyman's Library

A list of acknowledgments to copyright owners appears at the back
of this volume.

All rights reserved under International and Pan-American Copyright
Conventions. Published in the United States by Alfred A. Knopf,
a division of Random House, Inc., New York, and simultaneously in
Canada by Random House of Canada Limited, Toronto. Distributed
by Random House, Inc., New York. Published in the United Kingdom
by Everyman's Library, Northburgh House, 10 Northburgh Street,
London EC1V 0AT. Distributed by Random House (UK) Ltd.

US website: www.randomhouse.com/everymans

ISBN 1-4000-4356-5 (US)
1-84159-765-1 (UK)

A CIP catalogue record for this book is available from the British Library

Library of Congress Cataloging-in-Publication Data
Motherhood: poems about mothers / selected and edited by Carmela Ciuraru.
p. cm.—(Everyman's Library pocket poets)
Includes index.
ISBN 1-4000-4356-5 (alk. paper)
1. Mothers—Poetry. 2. Motherhood—Poetry. I. Ciuraru, Carmela.
II. Series.
PN6110.M64M68 2005   2004059986
808.81'9352—dc22

Typography by Peter B. Willberg
Typeset in the UK by AccComputing, North Barrow, Somerset
Printed and bound in Germany by GGP Media GmbH, Pössneck

CONTENTS

MOTHER AND DAUGHTER

6

ABSENCE AND LOSS

FOREWORD

The more than one hundred poems collected here share the theme of motherhood, yet each evokes a wholly singular experience. Christina Rossetti recalls her mother's love as a flame "whose blessed glow transcends the laws/Of time and change and mortal life and death." Jane Kenyon expresses a fear of abandonment: "Sometimes when she goes downtown, I think she will not come back." Anne Sexton describes the pure joy and safety of her mother's lap: "Your legs that bounce me up and down,/your dear nylon-covered legs,/are the horses I will ride/into eternity." Ruth Fainlight's memories are stirred by the smell of her mother's old handbag, still containing war letters from Fainlight's father, along with "mints/and lipstick and Coty powder." Jorie Graham describes keeping her mother's sewing box "in an old cookie tin, because/things last longer/in the dark."

While some poets reflect on the difficult legacies their mothers have left behind, others – including Louise Glück, Sharon Olds, and Eavan Boland – describe becoming mothers themselves. (As Oscar Wilde famously wrote, "All women become like their mothers. That is their tragedy. No man does. That's his.")

Several poems address the experience of childbirth. "Haste, infant bud of being, haste to blow!" implores the eighteenth-century poet Anna Laetitia Barbauld in "To a Little Invisible Being Who is Expected Soon to Become Visible." Louis MacNeice's startling "Prayer Before Birth" is a plaintive cry from the womb: "I am not yet born, console me."

Along with poems about mothers and daughters are those about mothers and sons: "Well, son, I'll tell you:/ Life for me ain't been no crystal stair," writes Langston Hughes in "Mother to Son." There are intimate tributes to mothers from such poets as Carolyn Kizer and Yehuda Amichai, as well as odes to grandmothers – influential figures who, in some instances, serve as primary caregivers. In "Among Women," Marie Ponsot recalls her formidable grandmother: "She looked fragile but had/High blood, runner's ankles,/Could endure, endure."

Finally – inevitably – is a section dealing with absence and loss, as in Patrick Kavanagh's defiant "In Memory of My Mother": "I do not think of you lying in the wet clay/Of a Monaghan graveyard; I see/You walking down a lane among the poplars/On your way to the station, or happily/Going to second Mass on a summer Sunday." Or E. E. Cummings' jubilant "if there are any heavens my mother will (all by/herself) have/one."

Whether conveying ambivalence, tenderness, resentment, or devotion, each poet in this anthology explores

14

the profound complexity of the mother–child relationship. And each poem seems, ultimately, a tribute to the experience of motherhood.

A final note: for their generous help, thanks are due to Alice Quinn, Colin Cundy, Sarah Fitzharding, and the staff of the *New Yorker* library.

Carmela Ciuraru

MOTHER AND BABY

TO A LITTLE INVISIBLE BEING WHO IS EXPECTED SOON TO BECOME VISIBLE

Germ of new life, whose powers expanding slow
For many a moon their full perfection wait, –
Haste, precious pledge of happy love, to go
Auspicious borne through life's mysterious gate.

What powers lie folded in thy curious frame, –
Senses from objects locked, and mind from thought!
How little canst thou guess thy lofty claim
To grasp at all the worlds the Almighty wrought!

And see, the genial season's warmth to share,
Fresh younglings shoot, and opening roses glow!
Swarms of new life exulting fill the air, –
Haste, infant bud of being, haste to blow!

For thee the nurse prepares her lulling songs,
The eager matrons count the lingering day;
But far the most thy anxious parent longs
On thy soft cheek a mother's kiss to lay.

She only asks to lay her burden down,
That her glad arms that burden may resume;
And nature's sharpest pangs her wishes crown,
That free thee living from thy living tomb.

She longs to fold to her maternal breast
Part of herself, yet to herself unknown;
To see and to salute the stranger guest,
Fed with her life through many a tedious moon.

Come, reap thy rich inheritance of love!
Bask in the fondness of a Mother's eye!
Nor wit nor eloquence her heart shall move
Like the first accents of thy feeble cry.

Haste, little captive, burst thy prison doors!
Launch on the living world, and spring to light!
Nature for thee displays her various stores,
Opens her thousand inlets of delight.

If charmed verse or muttered prayers had power,
With favouring spells to speed thee on thy way,
Anxious I'd bid my beads each passing hour,
Till thy wished smile thy mother's pangs o'erpay.

INFANT SORROW

My mother groaned, my father wept.
Into the dangerous world I leapt:
Helpless, naked, piping loud,
Like a fiend hid in a cloud.

Struggling in my father's hands,
Striving against my swaddling bands,
Bound and weary, I thought best
To sulk upon my mother's breast.

"THE ANGEL THAT PRESIDED O'ER MY BIRTH"

The Angel that presided o'er my birth
Said, "Little creature, form'd of Joy and Mirth,
Go love without the help of any Thing on Earth."

BEFORE THE BIRTH OF ONE OF HER CHILDREN

All things within this fading world hath end,
Adversity doth still our joys attend;
No ties so strong, no friends so dear and sweet,
But with death's parting blow is sure to meet.
The sentence past is most irrevocable,
A common thing, yet oh, inevitable.
How soon, my Dear, death may my steps attend,
How soon't may be thy lot to lose thy friend,
We both are ignorant, yet love bids me
These farewell lines to recommend to thee,
That when that knot's untied that made us one,
I may seem thine, who in effect am none.
And if I see not half my days that's due,
What nature would, God grant to yours and you;
The many faults that well you know I have
Let be interred in my oblivious grave;
If any worth or virtue were in me,
Let that live freshly in thy memory
And when thou feel'st no grief, as I no harms,
Yet love thy dead, who long lay in thine arms.
And when thy loss shall be repaid with gains
Look to my little babes, my dear remains.
And if thou love thyself, or loved'st me,
These O protect from step-dame's injury.

And if chance to thine eyes shall bring this verse,
With some sad sighs honour my absent hearse;
And kiss this paper for thy love's dear sake,
Who with salt tears this last farewell did take.

"UPON HER SOOTHING BREAST"

Upon her soothing breast
She lulled her little child;
A winter sunset in the west,
A dreary glory smiled.

FREIGHT

I am the ship in which you sail,
little dancing bones,
your passage between the dream
and the waking dream,
your sieve, your pea-green boat.
I'll pay whatever toll your ferry needs.
And you, whose history's already charted
in a rope of cells, be tender to
those other unnamed vessels
who will surprise you one day,
tug-tugging, irresistible,
and float you out beyond your depth,
where you'll look down, puzzled, amazed.

YOU'RE

Clownlike, happiest on your hands,
Feet to the stars, and moon-skulled,
Gilled like a fish. A common-sense
Thumbs-down on the dodo's mode.
Wrapped up in yourself like a spool,
Trawling your dark as owls do.
Mute as a turnip from the Fourth
Of July to All Fools' Day,
O high-riser, my little loaf.

Vague as fog and looked for like mail.
Farther off than Australia.
Bent-backed Atlas, our traveled prawn.
Snug as a bud and at home
Like a sprat in a pickle jug.
A creel of eels, all ripples.
Jumpy as a Mexican bean.
Right, like a well-done sum.
A clean slate, with your own face on.

MORNING SONG

Love set you going like a fat gold watch.
The midwife slapped your footsoles, and your bald cry
Took its place among the elements.

Our voices echo, magnifying your arrival. New statue.
In a drafty museum, your nakedness
Shadows our safety. We stand round blankly as walls.

I'm no more your mother
Than the cloud that distills a mirror to reflect its
    own slow
Effacement at the wind's hand.

All night your moth-breath
Flickers among the flat pink roses. I wake to listen:
A far sea moves in my ear.

One cry, and I stumble from bed, cow-heavy and floral
In my Victorian nightgown.
Your mouth opens clean as a cat's. The window square

Whitens and swallows its dull stars. And now you try
Your handful of notes;
The clear vowels rise like balloons.

CHILD

Your clear eye is the one absolutely beautiful thing.
I want to fill it with color and ducks,
The zoo of the new

Whose names you meditate –
April snowdrop, Indian pipe,
Little

Stalk without wrinkle,
Pool in which images
Should be grand and classical

Not this troublous
Wringing of hands, this dark
Ceiling without a star.

AN IMPROMPTU FOR ANN JENNINGS

Sing, memory, sing those seasons in the freezing
    suburb of Fern Tree, a rock-shaded place
with tree ferns, gullies, snowfalls and eye-pleasing
    prospects from paths along the mountain-face.

Nursing our babies by huge fires of wattle,
    or pushing them in prams when it was fine,
exchanging views on diet, or Aristotle,
    discussing Dr Spock or Wittgenstein,

cleaning up infants and the floors they muddied,
    bandaging, making ends and tempers meet –
sometimes I'd mind your children while you studied,
    or you'd take mine when I felt near defeat;

keeping our balance somehow through the squalling
    disorder, or with anguish running wild
when sickness, a sick joke from some appalling
    orifice of the nightwatch, touched a child;

think of it, woman: each of us gave birth to
    four children, our new lords whose beautiful
tyrannic kingdom might restore the earth to
    that fullness we thought lost beyond recall

when, in the midst of life, we could not name it,
    when spirit cried in darkness, *"I will have..."*
but what? have what? There was no word to frame it,
    though spirit beat at flesh as in a grave

from which it could not rise. But we have risen.
    Caesar's we were, and wild, though we seemed tame.
Now we move where we will. Age is no prison
    to hinder those whose joy has found its name.

We are our own. All Caesar's debts are rendered
    in full to Caesar. Time has given again
a hundredfold those lives that we surrendered,
    the love, the fruitfulness; but not the pain.

Before the last great fires we two went climbing
    like gods or blessed spirits in summer light
with the quiet pulse of mountain water chiming
    as if twenty years were one long dreaming night,

above the leafy dazzle of the streams
    to fractured rock, where water had its birth,
and stood in silence, at the roots of dreams,
    content to know: our children walk the earth.

NOW THAT I AM FOREVER WITH CHILD

How the days went
While you were blooming within me
I remember each upon each –
The swelling changed planes of my body –
And how you first fluttered, then jumped
And I thought it was my heart.

How the days wound down
And the turning of winter
I recall, with you growing heavy
Against the wind. I thought
Now her hands
Are formed, and her hair
Has started to curl
Now her teeth are done
Now she sneezes.
Then the seed opened.
I bore you one morning just before spring –
My head rang like a firey piston
My legs were towers between which
A new world was passing.

From then
I can only distinguish
One thread within running hours
You ... flowing through selves
Toward you.

AUDRE LORDE   31

THE NEW-BORN BABY'S SONG

When I was twenty inches long,
I could not hear the thrushes' song;
The radiance of morning skies
Was most displeasing to my eyes.

For loving looks, caressing words,
I cared no more than sun or birds;
But I could bite my mother's breast,
And that made up for all the rest.

ULTRASOUND
(*for Duncan*)

I ULTRASOUND
Oh whistle and I'll come to ye,
my lad, my wee shilpit ghost
summonsed from tomorrow.

Second sight,
a seer's mothy flicker,
an inner sprite:

this is what I see
with eyes closed;
a keek-aboot among secrets.

If Pandora
could have scanned
her dark box,

and kept it locked –
this ghoul's skull, punched eyes
is tiny Hope's,

hauled silver-quick
in a net of sound,
then, for pity's sake, lowered.

II SOLSTICE

To whom do I talk, an unborn thou,
sleeping in a bone creel.

Look what awaits you:
stars, milk-bottles, frost
on a broken outhouse roof

Let's close the door,
and rearrange
the dark red curtain.

Can you tell the days are opening,
admit a touch more light,
just a touch more?

III THAW

When we brought you home in a taxi
through the steel-grey thaw
after the coldest week in memory
– even the river sealed itself –
it was I, hardly breathing,
who came through the passage to our yard
welcoming our simplest things:
a chopping block, the frost-
split lintels; and though it meant a journey
through darkening snow,
arms laden with you in a blanket,

I had to walk to the top of the garden,
to touch, in a complicit
homage of equals, the spiral
trunks of our plum trees, the moss,
the robin's roost in the holly.
Leaning back on the railway wall,
I tried to remember;
but even my footprints were being erased
and the rising stars of Orion
denied what I knew: that as we were
hurled on a trolley through swing doors to theatre
they'd been there, aligned on the ceiling,
    ablaze with concern
for that difficult giving,
before we were two, from my one.

IV FEBRUARY
To the heap of nappies
carried from the automatic
in a red plastic basket

to the hanging out, my mouth
crowded with pegs;
to the notched prop

hoisting the wash,
a rare flight of swans,
hills still courying snow;

to spring's hint sailing
the westerly, snowdrops
sheltered by rowans –

to the day of St Bride, the first
sweet-wild weeks of your life
I willingly surrender.

V BAIRNSANG
Wee toshie man,
          gean tree and rowan
gif ye could staun
yer feet wad lichtsome tread
granite an saun,
but ye cannae yet staun
sae maun courie tae ma airm
an greetna, girna, Gretna Green

Peedie wee lad
          saumon, siller haddie
gin ye could rin
ye'd rin richt easy-strang
ower causey an carse,
but ye cannae yet rin
sae maun jist courie in
and fashna, fashna, Macrahanish Sand

Bonny wee boy
            peeswheep an whaup
gin ye could sing, yer sang
wad be caller
as a lauchin mountain burn
but ye cannae yet sing
sae maun courie tae ma hert
an grieve nat at aa, Ainster an Crail

My ain tottie bairn
            sternie an lift
gin ye could daunce, yer daunce
wad be that o life itsel,
but ye cannae yet daunce
sae maun courie in my erms
and sleep, saftly sleep, Unst and Yell

VI SEA URCHIN

Between my breast
and cupped hand,
            your head

rests as tenderly
as once I may
            have freighted

water, or drawn
treasure, whole
                    from a rockpool

with no premonition
of when next I find one
cast up
                    broken.

VII PRAYER

Our baby's heart, on the sixteen-week scan
was a fluttering bird, held in cupped hands.

I thought of St Kevin, hands opened in prayer
and a bird of the hedgerow nesting there,

and how he'd borne it, until the young had flown
– and I prayed: this new heart must outlive my own.

Scots words in Ultrasound
I: *shilpit:* pale; *keek-aboot:* peeping.
II: *creel:* basket.
V: *toshie:* tidy; *gean:* cherry; *courie tae:* nestle into; *greetna:*
don't cry; *girna:* don't whimper; *peedie:* tiny; *siller haddie:*
silver haddock; *causey:* causeway; *carse:* flat land near a river;
fashna: don't vex yourself; *peeswheep:* peewit, lapwing: *whaup:*
curlew; *caller:* fresh; *sternie:* star; *lift:* sky.

NIGHT LIGHT

Only your plastic night light dusts its pink
on the backs and undersides of things; your mother,
head resting on the nightside of one arm,
floats a hand above your cradle
to feel the humid tendril of your breathing.
Outside, the night rocks, murmurs ... Crouched
in this eggshell light, I feel my heart
slowing, opened to your tiny flame

as if your blue irises mirrored me
as if your smile breathed and warmed
and curled in your face which is only asleep.
There is space between me, I know,
and you. I hang above you like a planet –
you're a planet, too. One planet loves the other.

ANN WINTERS   39

PRAYER BEFORE BIRTH

I am not yet born; O hear me.
Let not the bloodsucking bat or the rat or the stoat or the
    clubfooted ghoul come near me.

I am not yet born, console me.
I fear that the human race may with tall walls wall me,
    with strong drugs dope me, with wise lies lure me,
        on black racks rack me, in blood-baths roll me.

I am not yet born; provide me
With water to dandle me, grass to grow for me, trees to
    talk to me, sky to sing to me, birds and a white light
        in the back of my mind to guide me.

I am not yet born; forgive me
For the sins that in me the world shall commit, my words
    When they speak me, my thoughts when they think me,
        my treason engendered by traitors beyond me,
            my life when they murder by means of my
                hands, my death when they live me.

I am not yet born; rehearse me
In the parts I must play and the cues I must take when
    old men lecture me, bureaucrats hector me, mountains
        frown at me, lovers laugh at me, the white

waves call me to folly and the desert calls
　　me to doom and the beggar refuses
　　　my gift and my children curse me.

I am not yet born; O hear me,
Let not the man who is beast or who thinks he is God
　come near me.

I am not yet born: O fill me
With strength against those who would freeze my
　humanity, would dragoon me into a lethal automaton,
　　would make me a cog in a machine, a thing with
　　　one face, a thing, and against all those
　　　who would dissipate my entirety, would
　　　　blow me like thistledown hither and
　　　　　thither or hither and thither
　　　　　like water held in the
　　　　　hands would spill me.

Let them not make me a stone and let them not spill me.
Otherwise kill me.

CHILDBIRTH

When, on the bearing mother, death's
Door opened its furious inch,
Instant of struggling and blood,
The commonplace became so strange

There was not looking at table or chair:
Miracle struck out the brain
Of order and ordinary: bare
Onto the heart the earth dropped then

With whirling quarters, the axle cracked,
Through that miracle-breached bed
All the dead could have got back;
With shriek and heave and spout of blood

The huge-eyed looming horde from
Under the floor of the heart, that run
To the madman's eye-corner came
Deafening towards light, whereon

A child whimpered upon the bed,
Frowning ten-toed ten-fingered birth
Put the skull back about the head
Righted the stagger of the earth.

MOTHER AND
DAUGHTER

THE POMEGRANATE

The only legend I have ever loved is
The story of a daughter lost in hell.
And found and rescued there.
Love and blackmail are the gist of it.
Ceres and Persephone the names.
And the best thing about the legend is
I can enter it anywhere. And have.
As a child in exile in
A city of fogs and strange consonants,
I read it first and at first I was
An exiled child in the crackling dusk of
The underworld, the stars blighted. Later
I walked out in a summer twilight
Searching for my daughter at bedtime.
When she came running I was ready
To make any bargain to keep her.
I carried her back past whitebeams.
And wasps and honey-scented buddleias.
But I was Ceres then and I knew
Winter was in store for every leaf
On every tree on that road.
Was inescapable for each one we passed.
And for me.
It is winter
And the stars are hidden.
I climb the stairs and stand where I can see

My child asleep beside her teen magazines,
Her can of Coke, her plate of uncut fruit.
The pomegranate! How did I forget it?
She could have come home and been safe
And ended the story and all
Our heartbroken searching but she reached
Out a hand and plucked a pomegranate.
She put out her hand and pulled down
The French sound for apple and
The noise of stone and the proof
That even in the place of death,
At the heart of legend, in the midst
Of rocks full of unshed tears
Ready to be diamonds by the time
The story was told, a child can be
Hungry. I could warn her. There is still a chance.
The rain is cold. The road is flint-coloured.
The suburb has cars and cable television.
The veiled stars are above ground.
It is another world. But what else
Can a mother give her daughter but such
Beautiful rifts in time?
If I defer the grief I will diminish the gift.
The legend must be hers as well as mine.
She will enter it. As I have.
She will wake up. She will hold
The papery, flushed skin in her hand.
And to her lips. I will say nothing.

A FABLE

Two women with
the same claim
came to the feet of
the wise king. Two women,
but only one baby.
The king knew
someone was lying.
What he said was
Let the child be
cut in half; that way
no one will go
empty-handed. He
drew his sword.
Then, of the two
women, one
renounced her share:
this was
the sign, the lesson.
Suppose
you saw your mother
torn between two daughters:
what could you do
to save her but be
willing to destroy
yourself – she would know

who was the rightful child,
the one who couldn't bear
to divide the mother.

A MOTHER'S PICTURE

A lady, the loveliest ever the sun
Looked down upon you must paint for me:
Oh, if I only could make you see
The clear blue eyes, the tender smile,
The sovereign sweetness, the gentle grace,
The woman's soul, and the angel's face
That are beaming on me all the while,
I need not speak these foolish words:
Yet one word tells you all I would say, –
She is my mother: you will agree
That all the rest may be thrown away.

ALICE CARY

TO MY MOTHER
(*Written in her sixteenth year*)

O thou whose care sustained my infant years,
And taught my prattling lip each note of love;
Whose soothing voice breathed comfort to my fears,
And round my brow hope's brightest garland wove;

To thee my lay is due, the simple song,
Which Nature gave me at life's opening day;
To thee these rude, these untaught strains belong,
Whose heart indulgent will not spurn my lay.

O say, amid this wilderness of life,
What bosom would have throbbed like thine for me?
Who would have smiled responsive? – who in grief,
Would e'er have felt, and feeling, grieved like thee?

Who would have guarded, with a falcon eye,
Each trembling footstep or each sport of fear?
Who would have marked my bosom bounding high,
And clasped me to her heart, with love's bright tear?

Who would have hung around my sleepless couch,
And fanned, with anxious hand, my burning brow?
Who would have fondly pressed my fevered lip,
In all the agony of love and woe?

50

None but a mother – none but one like thee,
Whose bloom has faded in the midnight watch;
Whose eye, for me, has lost its witchery,
Whose form has felt disease's mildew touch.

Yes, thou hast lighted me to health and life,
By the bright lustre of thy youthful bloom –
Yes, thou hast wept so oft o'er every grief,
That woe hath traced thy brow with marks of gloom.

O then, to thee, this rude and simple song,
Which breathes of thankfulness and love for thee,
To thee, my mother, shall this lay belong,
Whose life is spent in toil and care for me.

MOTHER AND DAUGHTER

She will not have it that my day wanes low,
    Poor of the fire its drooping sun denies,
    That on my brow the thin lines write good-byes
Which soon may be read plain for all to know,
Telling that I have done with youth's brave show;
    Alas! and done with youth in heart and eyes,
    With wonder and with far expectancies,
Save but to say "I knew such long ago."

She will not have it. Loverlike to me,
    She with her happy gaze finds all that's best,
She sees this fair and that unfretted still,
    And her own sunshine over all the rest:
So she half keeps me as she'd have me be,
And I forget to age, through her sweet will.

MY MOTHER'S KISS

My mother's kiss, my mother's kiss,
I feel its impress now;
As in the bright and happy days
She pressed it on my brow.

You say it is a fancied thing
Within my memory fraught;
To me it has a sacred place –
The treasure house of thought.

Again, I feel her fingers glide
Amid my clustering hair;
I see the love-light in her eyes,
When all my life was fair.

Again, I hear her gentle voice
In warning or in love.
How precious was the faith that taught
My soul of things above.

The music of her voice is stilled,
Her lips are paled in death.
As precious pearls I'll clasp her words
Until my latest breath.

The world has scattered round my path
Honor and wealth and fame;
But naught so precious as the thoughts
That gather round her name.

And friends have placed upon my brow
The laurels of renown;
But she first taught me how to wear
My manhood as a crown.

My hair is silvered o'er with age,
I'm longing to depart;
To clasp again my mother's hand,
And be a child at heart.

To roam with her the glory-land
Where saints and angels greet;
To cast our crowns with songs of love
At our Redeemer's feet.

NEWS FOR HER MOTHER

One mile more is
Where your door is,
   Mother mine! –
Harvest's coming,
Mills are strumming,
   Apples fine,
And the cider made to-year will be as wine.

Yet, not viewing
What's a-doing
   Here around
Is it thrills me,
And so fills me
   That I bound
Like a ball or leaf or lamb along the ground.

Tremble not now
At your lot now,
   Silly soul!
Hosts have sped them
Quick to wed them,
   Great and small,
Since the first two sighing half-hearts made a whole.

Yet I wonder,
Will it sunder
        Her from me?
Will she guess that
I said "Yes," – that
        His I'd be,
Ere I thought she might not see him as I see!

Old brown gable,
Granary, stable,
        Here you are!
O my mother,
Can another
        Ever bar
Mine from thy heart, make thy nearness seem afar?

SOMETHING

Resting her on my chest like a sleeping cat
I cannot recall my older daughter so small and new
and fear the memory of this
complete, absolute *something* will grow away
and fear the hand will never remember
stroking her head as she nursed
or fear I'll forget her soft cry
when I look up from sleep and see you lift her,
4 am, the curtains blowing in and out of the window
as the whole house breathes.

KIMIKO HAHN

FIRST THANKSGIVING

When she comes back, from college, I will see
the skin of her upper arms, cool,
matte, glossy. She will hug me, my old
soupy chest against her breasts,
I will smell her hair! She will sleep in this apartment,
her sleep like an untamed, good object, like a
soul in a body. She came into my life the
second great arrival, fresh
from the other world – which lay, from within him,
within me. Those nights, I fed her to sleep,
week after week, the moon rising,
and setting, and waxing – whirling, over the months,
in a steady blur, around our planet.
Now she doesn't need love like that, she has
had it. She will walk in glowing, we will talk,
and then, when she's fast asleep, I'll exult
to have her in that room again,
behind that door! As a child, I caught
bees, by the wings, and held them, some seconds,
looked into their wild faces,
listened to them sing, then tossed them back
into the air – I remember the moment the
arc of my toss swerved, and they entered
the corrected curve of their departure.

BLACK MOTHER WOMAN

I cannot recall you gentle.
Through your heavy love
I have become
an image of your once delicate flesh
split with deceitful longings.
When strangers come and compliment me
your aged spirit takes a bow
jingling with pride
but once you hid that secret
in the center of furies
hanging me
with deep breasts and wiry hair
with your own split flesh and long suffering eyes
buried in myths of no worth.

But I have peeled away your anger
down to its core of love
and look mother
I am
a dark temple where your true spirit rises
beautiful and tough as a chestnut
stanchion against your nightmares of weakness
and if my eyes conceal
a squadron of conflicting rebellions
I learned from you
to define myself
through your denials.

ALL HALLOWS EVE

My mother taught each one of us
to pray
as soon as we could talk
and every Halloween
to comfort us
before she went to work
my mother cooked fresh pumpkin with brown sugar
and placing penny candles in our windows
she said her yearly prayers
for all our dead.

As soon as mother left us
we feasted on warm pumpkin
until the empty pot sang out its earthy smell
and then, our mouths free,
we told each other stories of other Halloweens
making our wishes true
while from our windows
we watched the streets grow dark
and the witches slowly gathering below.

In each window
a penny candle in its own dish of water
flickered around our tales
throughout the evening.

Most of them burnt down
before our stories ended
and we went to bed
without replacing them.

LITTLE GIRL, MY STRING BEAN,
MY LOVELY WOMAN

My daughter, at eleven
(almost twelve), is like a garden.

Oh, darling! Born in that sweet birthday suit
and having owned it and known it for so long,
now you must watch high noon enter –
noon, that ghost hour.
Oh, funny little girl – this one under a blueberry sky,
this one! How can I say that I've known
just what you know and just where you are?

It's not a strange place, this odd home
where your face sits in my hand
so full of distance,
so full of its immediate fever.
The summer has seized you,
as when, last month in Amalfi, I saw
lemons as large as your desk-side globe –
that miniature map of the world –
and I could mention, too,
the market stalls of mushrooms
and garlic buds all engorged.
Or I think even of the orchard next door,
where the berries are done

and the apples are beginning to swell.
And once, with our first backyard,
I remember I planted an acre of yellow beans
we couldn't eat.

Oh, little girl,
my string bean,
how do you grow?
You grow this way.
You are too many to eat.

I hear
as in a dream
the conversation of the old wives
speaking of *womanhood.*
I remember that I heard nothing myself.
I was alone.
I waited like a target.

Let high noon enter –
the hour of the ghosts.
Once the Romans believed
that noon was the ghost hour,
and I can believe it, too,

under that startling sun,
and someday they will come to you,
someday, men bare to the waist, young Romans
at noon where they belong,
with ladders and hammers
while no one sleeps.

But before they enter
I will have said,
Your bones are lovely,
and before their strange hands
there was always this hand that formed.

Oh, darling, let your body in,
let it tie you in,
in comfort.
What I want to say, Linda,
is that women are born twice.

If I could have watched you grow
as a magical mother might,
if I could have seen through my magical transparent
      belly,
there would have been such ripening within:
your embryo,
the seed taking on its own,
life clapping the bedpost,
bones from the pond,

thumbs and two mysterious eyes,
the awfully human head,
the heart jumping like a puppy,
the important lungs,
the becoming –
while it becomes!
as it does now,
a world of its own,
a delicate place.

I say hello
to such shakes and knockings and high jinks,
such music, such sprouts,
such dancing-mad-bears of music,
such necessary sugar,
such goings-on!

Oh, little girl,
my string bean,
how do you grow?
You grow this way.
You are too many to eat.

What I want to say, Linda,
is that there is nothing in your body that lies.
All that is new is telling the truth.
I'm here, that somebody else,
an old tree in the background.

Darling,
stand still at your door,
sure of yourself, a white stone, a good stone –
as exceptional as laughter
you will strike fire,
that new thing!

THE BLOSSOM

A May morning. Light starting in the sky.
I have come here
after a long night.

The blossom on the apple tree is still in shadow,
its petals half white and filled with water at the core,
in which the secrecy and freshness of dawn are stored
even in the dark.

How much longer will I see girlhood in my daughter?

In other seasons,
I knew every leaf on this tree.
Now I stand here almost without seeing them

and so lost in grief
I hardly notice what is happening
as the light increases
and the blossom speaks

and turns to me with blond hair
and my eyebrows and says –

Imagine if I stayed here
even for the sake of your love.
What would happen to the summer? To the fruit?

Then holds out a dawn-soaked hand to me
whose fingers I counted at birth
years ago

and touches mine for the last time

and falls to earth.

WHAT SHALL I GIVE MY CHILDREN?

What shall I give my children? who are poor,
Who are adjudged the leastwise of the land,
Who are my sweetest lepers, who demand
No velvet and no velvety velour;
But who have begged me for a brisk contour,
Crying that they are quasi, contraband
Because unfinished, graven by a hand
Less than angelic, admirable or sure.
My hand is stuffed with mode, design, device.
But I lack access to my proper stone.
And plenitude of plan shall not suffice
Nor grief nor love shall be enough alone
To ratify my little halves who bear
Across an autumn freezing everywhere.

AFTER 37 YEARS MY MOTHER
APOLOGIZES FOR MY CHILDHOOD

When you tilted toward me, arms out
like someone trying to walk through a fire,
when you swayed toward me, crying out you were
sorry for what you had done to me, your
eyes filling with terrible liquid like
balls of mercury from a broken thermometer
skidding on the floor, when you quietly screamed
Where else could I turn? Who else did I have?, the
chopped crockery of your hands swinging toward me, the
water cracking from your eyes like moisture from
stones under heavy pressure, I could not
see what I would do with the rest of my life.
The sky seemed to be splintering, like a window
someone is bursting into or out of, your
tiny face glittered as if with
shattered crystal, with true regret, the
regret of the body. I could not see what my
days would be, with you sorry, with
you wishing you had not done it, the
sky falling around me, its shards
glistening in my eyes, your old, soft
body fallen against me in horror I
took you in my arms, I said *It's all right,
don't cry, it's all right*, the air filled with
flying glass, I hardly knew what I
said or who I would be now that I had forgiven you.

70   SHARON OLDS

UPON BEING AWAKENED AT NIGHT BY MY FOUR YEAR OLD DAUGHTER

When I consider, Thérèse,
The cricket in its shrill address,
Penetrating your warm, familiar room,
Ceaselessly proclaiming he means no harm:
Who begs release and begs release,

This orthopter in all its fury, Thérèse,
Knows more of fear than you possess,
You, bedded deep in your dense room,
While he, mysteriously bereft of stars – O cease!
Heralds – O won't he cease? – his doom.

Come! let us seek, Thérèse,
His self-imprisonment, and bless
Our certainty that this deep room
Conceals no giant who means you harm:
So mutually arrange our green release.

By your sleep again covered, Thérèse,
Innocent of stress your face marvelous
Lies, unsuspecting what I must confess:
Those things which me most terrify
I neither can hear nor touch nor see.

MOMMA SAYINGS

Momma had words for us:
We were "crumb crushers,"
"eating machines,"
"bottomless pits."
Still, she made us charter members
of the bonepickers' club,
saying, "Just don't let your eyes
get bigger than your stomachs."
Saying, "Take all you want,
but eat all you take."
Saying, "I'm not made of money, you know,
and the man at the Safeway
don't give away groceries for free."

She trained us not to leave lights on
"all over the house,"
because "electricity costs money –
so please turn the light off when you leave a room
and take the white man's hand out of my pocket."

When we were small
she called our feet "ant mashers,"
but when we'd outgrow our shoes,
our feet became "platforms."
She told us we must be growing big feet

to support some big heavyset women
(like our grandma Tiddly).

When she had to buy us new underwear
to replace the old ones full of holes,
she'd swear we were growing razor blades in
    our behinds,
"you tear these drawers up so fast."

Momma had words for us, alright:
She called us "the wrecking crew."
She said our untidy bedroom
looked like "a cyclone struck it."

Our dirty fingernails she called "victory gardens."
And when we'd come in from playing outside
she'd tell us, "You smell like iron rust."
She'd say, "Go take a bath
and get some of that funk off you."
But when the water ran too long in the tub
she'd yell, "That's enough water to wash an elephant."
And after the bath she'd say,
"Be sure and grease those ashy legs."
She'd lemon-cream our elbows
and pull the hot comb
through "these tough kinks on your heads."

Momma had lots of words for us,
her never quite perfect daughters,
the two brown pennies
she wanted to polish
so we'd shine like dimes.

GLEN COVE, 1957

A strawberry shortcake sits breathing sweetness
    on a cloud
  above the curvy cartoon fridge and I am seven
    climbing
phone books piled on a wobbly chair until the dull silver
  radiator looms, then a trickle and someone saying
cracked open. Am I dead? Am I an egg? I hatch out,
  bandaged under grapevines near a gullyful of trash.
The wooden lawn chair knits splinters into the
    backs of my
  knees and I will get no shortcake. Am I downcast or
defiant? This and so much else I reach for is gone –
  the color of the bulkhead being painted,
the kind of sandwiches my mother hands the splattered
  churchmen, and does she know she's pretty?
Rotten apples on spring ground are smeary bittersweet
  and I am the age of my daughter who still loves fog.
I hate it. The way last month's huge sadnesses and tiny
  triumphs are leaking onto her pillow as she sleeps,
and who knows which moments will get snagged
    and remain
  to point to who she's become once she's forgotten
the rest, her right foot asleep and her daughter
  gap-mouthed below her wide with the world.

ELLEN WATSON   75

DRAWING FROM THE PAST

Only Mama and I were at home.
We ate tomato sandwiches
with sweeps of mayonnaise
on indifferent white bread.

Surely it was September,
my older brother at school.
The tomatoes were fragrant
and richly red, perhaps the last
before frost.

I was alert to the joy of eating
sandwiches alone with Mama, bare
feet braced on the underpinnings
of the abraded kitchen table.

Once I'd made a mark in the wood
by pressing too hard as I traced
the outline of a horse.

I was no good at drawing – from life,
or from imagination. My brother
was good at it, and I was alert
to that, too.

MOTHER'S SEWING BOX

In an old cookie tin, because
things last longer
in the dark.
She needs to be left alone.
Here are saved
the bits of string
too small to save, the eyes
of the needles.
On the string
the knots are birds that sit,
that cannot leave. The buttons
are wheels. Assemble them,
these uneven machines,
and they say, *how much*
for Effort, or, *wait,*
I've changed my mind,
I want to come along.
To disobey
is to hide or to be
unmended. Maybe you'll find it,
she says after I've said
I don't have, didn't take,
her belongings.
The spools of thread
form a train. Swarms

of starling cry we are pins,
pins. We are going so fast.
Maybe you'll
find it, maybe
you'll find it, lazy susan
got a black eye. The needle,
covering its tracks,
makes a pattern
of its incisions, the pincushion
with its pocked body
snapped quills . . .
and if she isn't gone
she lives there still.

THE ONLY CHILD SENDS A GIFT TO
HER MOTHER

What came after me is the point – that one fall
night I arrived; an hour later the flowers; and never

another living child. I'm sorry to write it. Twenty-eight
     clever
years have come up with nothing between us. Even
     apart, I call

your late nights awake, the chrysanthemums on
     your table
the same as mine. Even from west to east, the change
     is no hour.

This very instant, my night is in bloom with your
     sounds;
the same sleeping girl is asleep in the same cradle;

your amber mums sketch themselves on my white
     paper.
I believe these are only all your thoughts in my words,

secret as soil. Your back-yard backlit trees are what
     I've just heard.
I write with your black pencil, not a second later.

ELIZABETH MACKLIN   79

THE FORTRESS
while taking a nap with Linda

Under the pink quilted covers
I hold the pulse that counts your blood.
I think the woods outdoors
are half asleep,
left over from summer
like a stack of books after a flood,
left over like those promises I never keep.
On the right, the scrub pine tree
waits like a fruit store
holding up bunches of tufted broccoli.

We watch the wind from our square bed.
I press down my index finger –
half in jest, half in dread –
on the brown mole
under your left eye, inherited
from my right cheek: a spot of danger
where a bewitched worm ate its way through our soul
in search of beauty. My child, since July
the leaves have been fed
secretly from a pool of beet-red dye.

And sometimes they are battle green
with trunks as wet as hunters' boots,

smacked hard by the wind, clean
as oilskins. No,
the wind's not off the ocean.
Yes, it cried in your room like a wolf
and your pony tail hurt you. That was a long time ago.
The wind rolled the tide like a dying
woman. She wouldn't sleep,
she rolled there all night, grunting and sighing.

Darling, life is not in my hands;
life with its terrible changes
will take you, bombs or glands,
your own child at
your breast, your own house on your own land.
Outside the bittersweet turns orange.
Before she died, my mother and I picked those fat
branches, finding orange nipples
on the gray wire strands.
We weeded the forest, curing trees like cripples.

Your feet thump-thump against my back
and you whisper to yourself. Child,
what are you wishing? What pact
are you making?

What mouse runs between your eyes? What ark
can I fill for you when the world goes wild?
The woods are underwater, their weeds are shaking
in the tide; birches like zebra fish
flash by in a pack.
Child, I cannot promise that you will get your wish.

I cannot promise very much.
I give you the images I know.
Lie still with me and watch.
A pheasant moves
by like a seal, pulled through the mulch
by his thick white collar. He's on show
like a clown. He drags a beige feather that he removed,
one time, from an old lady's hat.
We laugh and we touch.
I promise you love. Time will not take away that.

GENETIC EXPEDITION

Each evening I see my breasts
slacker, black-tipped
like the heavy plugs on hot water bottles;
each day resembling more the spiked fruits
dangling from natives in the *National Geographic*
my father forbade us to read.

Each morning I drip coffee onto my blouse
and tear into one slice of German bread,
thin layer of margarine, radishes, the years
spreading across my dark behind, even more
sumptuous after childbirth, the part of me
I swore to relish

always. My child has
her father's hips, his hair
like the miller's daughter, combed gold.
Though her lips are mine, housewives
stare when we cross the parking lot
because of that ghostly profusion.

You can't be cute, she says. *You're big.*
She's lost her toddler's belly,
that seaworthy prow. She regards me
with serious eyes, power-lit,

atomic gaze
I'm sucked into, sheer through to

the gray brain of sky.

THE MONTH OF JUNE: $13\frac{1}{2}$

As my daughter approaches graduation and
puberty at the same time, at her
own calm deliberate serious rate,
she begins to kick up her heels, jazz out her
hands, thrust out her hip-bones, chant
I'm great! I'm great! She feels 8th grade coming
open around her, a chrysalis cracking and
letting her out, it falls behind her and
joins the other husks on the ground,
7th grade, 6th grade, the
purple rind of 5th grade, the
hard jacket of 4th when she had so much pain,
3rd grade, 2nd, the dim cocoon of
1st grade back there somewhere on the path, and
kindergarten like a strip of thumb-suck blanket
taken from the actual blanket they wrapped her
    in at birth.
The whole school is coming off her shoulders like a
cloak unclasped, and she dances forth in her
jerky sexy child's joke dance of
self, self, her throat tight and a
hard new song coming out of it, while her
two dark eyes shine
above her body like a good mother and a
good father who look down and
love everything their baby does, the way she
lives their love.

SHARON OLDS   85

THE QUEEN AND THE YOUNG PRINCESS

Mother, mother, let me go
There are so many things I wish to do.
My child, the time is not yet ripe
You are not yet ready for life.
But what is my life that is to come to be?
Much the same, child, as it has been for me.
But Mother you often say you have a headache
Because of the crown you wear for duty's sake.
So it is, so it is, a headache I have
And that is what you must grow up to carry to the
     grave.
But in between Mother do you not enjoy the pleasant
     weather
And to see the bluebottle and the soft feather?
Ah my child, that joy you speak of must be a pleasure
Of human stature, not the measure
Of animals', who have no glorious duty
To perform, no headache and so cannot see beauty.
Up, child, up, embrace the headache and the crown
Marred pleasure's best, shadow makes the sun strong.

HUMAN AFFECTION

Mother, I love you so.
Said the child, I love you more than I know.
She laid her head on her mother's arm,
And the love between them kept them warm.

MOTHER AND SON

ON MY SON'S RETURN OUT OF ENGLAND, JULY 17, 1661

All praise to Him who hath now turned
My fears to joys, my sighs to song,
My tears to smiles, my sad to glad;
He's come for whom I waited long.

Thou didst preserve him as he went,
In raging storms didst safely keep,
Didst that ship bring to quiet port.
The other sank low in the deep.

From dangers great Thou didst him free
Of pirates who were near at hand,
And order'st so the adverse wind
That he before them got to land.

In country strange Thou didst provide,
And friends raised him in every place,
And courtesies of sundry sorts
From such as 'fore ne'er saw his face.

In sickness when he lay full sore,
His help and his physician wert.
When royal ones that time did die,
Thou healed'st his flesh and cheered his heart.

From trouble and encumbers Thou
Without all fraud didst set him free,
That without scandal he might come
To th'land of his nativity.

On eagles' wings him hither brought
Through want and dangers manifold,
And thus hath granted my request
That I Thy mercies might behold.

O help me pay Thy vows, O Lord,
That ever I may thankful be
And may put him in mind of what
Thou'st done for him, and so for me.

In both our hearts erect a frame
Of duty and of thankfulness,
That all Thy favours great received
Our upright walking may express.

O Lord, grant that I may never forget Thy loving
    kindness in this particular, and how graciously
    Thou hast answered my desires.

TO MY MOTHER

Most near, most dear, most loved and most far,
Under the window where I often found her
Sitting as huge as Asia, seismic with laughter,
Gin and chicken helpless in her Irish hand,
Irresistible as Rabelais, but most tender for
The lame dogs and hurt birds that surround her, –
She is a procession no one can follow after
But be like a little dog following a brass band.

She will not glance up at the bomber, or condescend
To drop her gin and scuttle to a cellar,
But lean on the mahogany table like a mountain
Whom only faith can move, and so I send
O all my faith and all my love to tell her
That she will move from mourning into morning.

THE LITTLE BLACK BOY

My mother bore me in the southern wild,
And I am black, but O! my soul is white;
White as an angel is the English child,
But I am black, as if bereav'd of light.

My mother taught me underneath a tree,
And sitting down before the heat of day,
She took me on her lap and kissed me,
And pointing to the east, began to say:

"Look on the rising sun! there God does live,
And gives his light and gives his heat away;
And flowers and trees and beasts and men receive
Comfort in morning, joy in the noon day.

"And we are put on earth a little space,
That we may learn to bear the beams of love;
And these black bodies and this sun-burnt face
Is but a cloud, and like a shady grove.

"For when our souls have learn'd the heat to bear,
The cloud will vanish; we shall hear his voice,
Saying: 'Come out from the grove, my love & care,
And round my golden tent like lambs rejoice.'"

Thus did my mother say, and kissed me;
And thus I say to little English boy:
When I from black and he from white cloud free,
And round the tent of God like lambs we joy,

I'll shade him from the heat, till he can bear
To lean in joy upon our father's knee;
And then I'll stand and stroke his silver hair,
And be like him, and he will then love me.

From POEMS TO A SON

Forget us, children. Our conscience
   need not belong to you.
You can be free to write the tale
   of your own days and passions.

Here in this family album
   lies the salt family of Lot.
It is for you to reckon up
   the many claims on Sodom.

You didn't fight your brothers
   my curly headed boy!
So this is your time, this is your day.
   The land is purely yours.

Sin, cross, quarrel, anger,
   these are ours. There have been
too many funerals held by now
   for an Eden you've never seen

whose fruit you never tasted.
   So now, put off your mourning.
Understand: they are blind
   who lead you, but then

our quarrel is not your quarrel,
    So as you rush from Meudon
and race to the Kuban
    children, prepare for battle

in the field of your own days.

MARINA TSVETAEVA

TRANSLATED BY ELAINE FEINSTEIN

SHARDS

You cannot leave your mother an orphan.   JOYCE

For me, deprived of fire and water,
Separated from my only son ...
Being on the infamous scaffold of misfortune
Is like being beneath the canopy of a throne ...

How well he's succeeded, this fierce debater,
All the way to the Yenisey plains ...
To you he's a vagabond, rebel, conspirator –
To me he is – an only son.

Seven thousand and three kilometers ...
Don't you hear your mother's call
In the north wind's frightful howl?
Cooped up, surrounded by adversity,
You grow wild there, you grow savage – you are dear,
You are the last and the first, you – are ours.
Over my Leningrad grave
Spring wanders indifferently.

When and to whom did I talk?
Why didn't I hide from people
That my son was rotting in the camps,
That they flogged my Muse to death.

I am more guilty than anyone on earth
Who ever was, is now, or ever will be.
And to lie about in a madhouse
Would be a great honor for me.

You raised me up, like a slain beast
On a bloody hook,
So that sniggering, and not believing,
Foreigners wandered in
And wrote in their respectable papers
That my incomparable gift had died out,
That I had been a poet among poets,
But my thirteenth hour had struck.

ANNA AKHMATOVA   99
TRANSLATED BY JUDITH HEMSCHEMEYER

ON A SON RETURNED TO NEW ZEALAND

He is my green branch growing in a far plantation.
He is my first invention.

No one can be in two places at once.
So we left Athens on the same morning.
I was in a hot railway carriage, crammed
between Serbian soldiers and peasant
women, on sticky seats, with nothing to
drink but warm mineral water.
                                 He was
in a cabin with square windows, sailing
across the Mediterranean, fast,
to Suez.
             Then I was back in London
in the tarnished summer, remembering,
as I folded his bed up, and sent the
television set away. Letters came
from Aden and Singapore, late.
                                 He was
already in his father's house, on the
cliff-top, where the winter storms roll across
from Kapiti Island, and the flax bends
before the wind. He could go no further.

He is my bright sea-bird on a rocky beach.

MOTHER AND CHILD

Theirs is the bond
Demonstrable. Authority
In the blood
Still rebuilding
The baffling hierarchies
Of mother and child
To shield her
From time, from open
Time ...

                something grows
Outward from forgotten roots,
Best forgotten, growing
Like the black branch
Out into space
From the incurable root, the most living
Green tip fed by a sap
The great black mass brings it, leafing
From the thin twig in new space.

ILLUMINATIONS

My son squats in the snow in his blue snowsuit.
All around him stubble, the brown
degraded bushes. In the morning air
they seem to stiffen into words.
And, between, the white steady silence.
A wren hops on the airstrip
under the sill, drills
for sustenance, then spreads
its short wings, shadows
dropping from them.

Last winter he could barely speak.
I moved his crib to face the window:
in the dark mornings
he would stand and grip the bars
until the walls appeared,
calling *light*, *light*,
that one syllable, in
demand or recognition.

He sits at the kitchen window
with his cup of apple juice.
Each tree forms where he left it,
leafless, trapped in his breath.
How clear their edges are,

no limb obscured by motion,
as the sun rises
cold and single over the map of language.

MOTHER TO SON

Well, son, I'll tell you:
Life for me ain't been no crystal stair.
It's had tacks in it,
And splinters,
And boards torn up,
And places with no carpet on the floor –
Bare.
But all the time
I'se been a-climbin' on,
And reachin' landin's,
And turnin' corners,
And sometimes goin' in the dark
Where there ain't been no light.
So boy, don't you turn back.
Don't you set down on the steps
'Cause you finds it's kinder hard.
Don't you fall now –
For I'se still goin', honey,
I'se still climbin',
And life for me ain't been no crystal stair.

PRE-TEXT
(*for Douglas, at one*)

Archaic, his gestures
hieratic, just like Caesar or Sappho
or Mary's Jesus or Ann's Mary or Jane
Austen once, or me or your mother's you

the sudden baby surges to his feet
and sways, head forward, chin high,
arms akimbo, hands dangling idle,
elbows up, as if winged.

The features of his face stand out
amazed, all eyes as his aped posture
sustains him aloft
                          a step a step a rush
and he walks,

Young Anyone, his lifted point of view
far beyond the calendar.

What time is it? Firm in time
he is out of date –

like a cellarer for altar wines
tasting many summers in one glass,

or like a grandmother
in whose womb her
granddaughter once
slept in egg inside
grandma's unborn daughter's
folded ovaries.

MOTHER, SUMMER, I

My mother, who hates thunderstorms,
Holds up each summer day and shakes
It out suspiciously, lest swarms
Of grape-dark clouds are lurking there;
But when the August weather breaks
And rains begin, and brittle frost
Sharpens the bird-abandoned air,
Her worried summer look is lost.

And I her son, though summer-born
And summer-loving, none the less
Am easier when the leaves are gone;
Too often summer days appear
Emblems of perfect happiness
I can't confront: I must await
A time less bold, less rich, less clear:
An autumn more appropriate.

CHIFFON MORNING

I

I am lying in bed with my mother,
where my father seldom lay. Little poem,
help me to say all I need to say, better.
Hair dyed, combed; nails polished; necklace-like scar
ear-to-ear; stocky peasant's bulk hidden
under an unfeminine nightgown; sour-milk
breaths rehearsing death, she faces me, her room
a pill museum where orange teabags
draining on napkins almost pass for art.
Even the Christmas amaryllis sags
under the weight of its blood red
petals, unfolding like a handkerchief.
From the television screen, a beauty-
pageant queen waves serenely at me.

II

In the oily black barbecue smoke,
in our blue Chevrolet station wagon,
in a cottage at the sea, no one spoke
but me to the nerveless God
who never once stopped their loveless act:
the cursing mouths, the shoving and choking,
the violent pulse, the wrecked hair, the hunchbacked
reprisal, the suddenly inverted sky,

the fiendish gasping, the blade that cuts all
understanding, the white knuckles, the fly
remarkably poised on a blue throat.
I try to pity them. Perhaps God did
on those occasions when battle was a prelude
to sex, and peace, like an arrow, found us.

III

How many nights did I throw my arms around
our black dog's neck and listen to Mother,
on her knees, retching supper? The love hound
licked my face again and again like fur.
Far off, the weirdly ethereal bells
of an ice cream truck, hypnotic in contrast,
calmed me like tapers burning steadily.
Near dawn, when she was pregnant with her last-
born, there were complications. The long path
to the ambulance was splashed with what came
from inside her, a floating purplish wax
our neighbor, a cheerful woman, mopped up.
When Mother came home thin again, the sun crowned
whom she cradled. Father was out of town.

IV

On the mowed grass, I once posed in black tie;
now a neighbor's labradors sow lawn-burn.
Pink dogwoods Mother and I transplanted
throw off their sentimental silks.
If squirrels nest in a tree too close by,
she hires a colonel's son to oust them.
No one calls except born-again women.
"Must you tell everyone what you are?"
she protests, during each of our visits;
I rake leaves and burn them like a corpse,
wondering if I'm better off without her –
like Father when he was a GI
and their trailer-park love got coffined up
in a suburban dream house, for sale now.

V

As the cuckoo clock crows in the kitchen,
on her nightstand others as bluntly chime,
but cannot break her drugged oblivion.
Please wake up, Mother, and wet your cottonmouth.
"She was agitated," nurses whispered
when we found her tied to the bed, knocked out.
Demerol blocked the pain, entering through the eyes,
while the mind, crushed like a wineglass, healed.
"I'll bury you all," she gloated, at home again.
Months later, they stitched her throat in surgery.

The voice that had been on the radio
when the war was on, plunged a tragic octave.
More pills crowded her daily glass of milk.
My guilt seemed vain compared to what she felt.

VI

Mother is naked and holding me up
above her as soap streams from my face
(I'm wearing a dumb ape's frown) into the tub
where she is seated: the mind replays
what nurtures it. The black months when she
would lie assassinated like our Siamese cat
are still far off. Yet, tranced by a lush light,
which no one else sees, like a leaden bee
shackled to a poppy, I am not free.
Each time I am dunked in the green, green
sacramental water, I glare shamelessly
as she shrieks and kisses me, gripped in air;
I do not know if she loves me or cares,
if it's suffering or joy behind her tears.

CROW AND MAMA

When Crow cried his mother's ear
Scorched to a stump.

When he laughed she wept
Blood her breasts her palms her brow all wept blood.

He tried a step, then a step, and again a step –
Every one scarred her face for ever.

When he burst out in rage
She fell back with an awful gash and a fearful cry.

When he stopped she closed on him like a book
On a bookmark, he had to get going.

He jumped into the car the towrope
Was around her neck he jumped out.

He jumped into the plane but her body was jammed
        in the jet –
There was a great row, the flight was cancelled.

He jumped into the rocket and its trajectory
Drilled clean through her heart he kept on

And it was cosy in the rocket, he could not see much
But he peered out through the portholes at Creation

And saw the stars millions of miles away
And saw the future and the universe

Opening and opening
And kept on and slept and at last

Crashed on the moon awoke and crawled out

Under his mother's buttocks.

MY MOTHER'S PEARS

Plump, green-gold, Worcester's pride,
transported through autumn skies
in a box marked "Handle With Care"

sleep eighteen Bartlett pears,
hand-picked and polished and packed
for deposit at my door,

each in its crinkled nest
with a stub of stem attached
and a single bright leaf like a flag.

A smaller than usual crop,
but still enough to share with me,
as always at harvest time.

Those strangers are my friends
whose kindness blesses the house
my mother built at the edge of town

beyond the last trolley-stop
when the century was young, and she
proposed, for her children's sake,

to marry again, not knowing how soon
the windows would grow dark
and the velvet drapes come down.

Rubble accumulates in the yard,
workmen are hammering on the roof,
I am standing knee-deep in dirt

with a shovel in my hand.
Mother has wrapped a kerchief round her head,
her glasses glint in the sun.

When my sisters appear on the scene,
gangly and softly tittering,
she waves them back into the house

to fetch us pails of water,
and they skip out of our sight
in their matching middy blouses.

I summon up all my strength
to set the pear tree in the ground,
unwinding its burlap shroud.

It is taller than I. "Make room
for the roots!" my mother cries,
"Dig the hole deeper."

STANLEY KUNITZ   115

AVE MARIA

Mothers of America
                    let your kids go to the movies!
get them out of the house so they won't know what
        you're up to
it's true that fresh air is good for the body
                            but what about the soul
that grows in darkness, embossed by silvery images
and when you grow old as grow old you must
                            they won't hate you
they won't criticize you they won't know
                        they'll be in some glamorous country
they first saw on a Saturday afternoon or playing hookey
they may even be grateful to you
                        for their first sexual experience
which only cost you a quarter
                        and didn't upset the peaceful home
they will know where candy bars come from
                        and gratuitous bags of popcorn
as gratuitous as leaving the movie before it's over
with a pleasant stranger whose apartment is in the
        Heaven on Earth Bldg
near the Williamsburg Bridge
            oh mothers you will have made the little tykes
so happy because if nobody does pick them up in the
        movies

they won't know the difference
            and if somebody does it'll be sheer gravy
and they'll have been truly entertained either way
instead of hanging around the yard
                        or up in their room
                                    hating you
prematurely since you won't have done anything
      horribly mean yet
except keeping them from the darker joys
                        it's unforgivable the latter
so don't blame me if you won't take this advice
                        and the family breaks up
and your children grow old and blind in front of a
      TV set
            seeing
movies you wouldn't let them see when they were young

THE HORSE SHOW

Constantly near you, I never in my entire
sixty-four years knew you so well as yesterday
or half so well. We talked. You were never
so lucid, so disengaged from all exigencies
of place and time. We talked of ourselves,
intimately, a thing never heard of between us.
How long have we waited? almost a hundred years.

You said, Unless there is some spark, some
spirit we keep within ourselves, life, a
continuing life's impossible – and it is all
we have. There is no other life, only the one.
The world of the spirits that comes afterward
is the same as our own, just like you sitting
there they come and talk to me, just the same.

They come to bother us. Why? I said. I don't
know. Perhaps to find out what we are doing.
Jealous, do you think? I don't know. I
don't know why they should want to come back.
I was reading about some men who had been
buried under a mountain, I said to her, and
one of them came back after two months,

digging himself out. It was in Switzerland,
you remember? Of course I remember. The
villagers tho't it was a ghost coming down
to complain. They were frightened. They
do come, she said, what you call
my "visions". I talk to them just as I
am talking to you. I see them plainly.

Oh if I could only read! You don't know
what adjustments I have made. All
I can do is to try to live over again
what I knew when your brother and you
were children — but I can't always succeed.
Tell me about the horse show. I have
been waiting all week to hear about it.

Mother darling, I wasn't able to get away.
Oh that's too bad. It was just a show;
they make the horses walk up and down
to judge them by their form. Oh is that
all? I tho't it was something else. Oh
they jump and run too. I wish you had been
there, I was so interested to hear about it.

WILLIAM CARLOS WILLIAMS   119

MOTHER'S THINGS

I wanted approval,
carrying with me
things of my mother's
beyond their use to me –

worn-out clock,
her small green lock box,
father's engraved brass plate
for printing calling cards –

such size of her still
calls out to me
with that silently
expressive will.

NICK AND THE CANDLESTICK

I am a miner. The light burns blue.
Waxy stalactites
Drip and thicken, tears

The earthen womb
Exudes from its dead boredom.
Black bat airs

Wrap me, raggy shawls,
Cold homicides.
They weld to me like plums.

Old cave of calcium
Icicles, old echoer.
Even the newts are white,

Those holy Joes.
And the fish, the fish –
Christ! they are panes of ice,

A vice of knives,
A piranha
Religion, drinking

Its first communion out of my live toes.
The candle
Gulps and recovers its small altitude,

Its yellows hearten.
O love, how did you get here?
O embryo

Remembering, even in sleep,
Your crossed position.
The blood blooms clean

In you, ruby.
The pain
You wake to is not yours.

Love, love,
I have hung our cave with roses,
With soft rugs –

The last of Victoriana.
Let the stars
Plummet to their dark address,

Let the mercuric
Atoms that cripple drip
Into the terrible well,

You are the one
Solid the spaces lean on, envious.
You are the baby in the barn.

MY SON THE MAN

Suddenly his shoulders get a lot wider,
the way Houdini would expand his body
while people were putting him in chains. It seems
no time since I would help him put on his sleeper,
guide his calves into the shadowy interior,
zip him up and toss him up and
catch his weight. I cannot imagine him
no longer a child, and I know I must get ready,
get over my fear of men now my son
is going to be one. This was not
what I had in mind when he pressed up through me
    like a
sealed trunk through the ice of the Hudson,
snapped the padlock, unsnaked the chains,
appeared in my arms. Now he looks at me
the way Houdini studied a box
to learn the way out, then smiled and let himself be
    manacled.

MOTHER OF THE GROOM

What she remembers
Is his glistening back
In the bath, his small boots
In the ring of boots at her feet.

Hands in her voided lap,
She hears a daughter welcomed.
It's as if he kicked when lifted
And slipped her soapy hold.

Once soap would ease off
The wedding ring
That's bedded forever now
In her clapping hand.

BROWN CIRCLE

My mother wants to know
why, if I hate
family so much,
I went ahead and
had one. I don't
answer my mother.
What I hated
was being a child,
having no choice about
what people I loved.

I don't love my son
the way I meant to love him.
I thought I'd be
the lover of orchids who finds
red trillium growing
in the pine shade, and doesn't
touch it, doesn't need
to possess it. What I am
is the scientist,
who comes to that flower
with a magnifying glass
and doesn't leave, though
the sun burns a brown
circle of grass around

the flower. Which is
more or less the way
my mother loved me.

I must learn
to forgive my mother,
now that I'm helpless
to spare my son.

MY MOTHER'S HANDS

Now that she's ashamed of their ancient burls and
      gibbous knobs –
"Don't be ashamed!" I helplessly cry –
I find myself staring at the raw matter of their
decay, nails crumbling to the opalescent grit
of their lunulae, liver spots speckling the blue dorsal vein
with its throbbing blue limbs, as if the leopard,
symbol of lust in Dante, lay panting, enfeebled,
in the dark wood.

I can't bear that these hands won't always be here,
though I barely noticed them when they were still
      dexterous,
commanding me to come here, do this chore, listen
      to this
sweet story, come here, sweetheart, come here . . .

Now a scythelike rod planted within the same index
      finger
gives it an incongruous come-hither look that forces
passersby to point to themselves, thinking
she's beckoning to them, an optical illusion, of course,
like the Beauty and the Crone.

"This hand is not the crux and matter of you,"
     I want to say,
but know she'd laugh and ask, "Is it what's the matter
with you?" or – worse – look away in pain, saying,
"It doesn't matter, it doesn't matter."

And so I hold on tight as she sits in her wheelchair, as if
to guide her somewhere, anywhere, until I kiss her
     goodbye,
and her hands fall from my own to a spot on her desk
by the glass paperweight that my father gave her
when they were young: clear, abstract, voluptuous,
with five sparkling air bubbles clutching
a bouquet of clouds.

PICNIC

When my father was three years dead and dying
away more quickly than other dead fathers do,
I took my mother in my 1935 green Ford
for a picnic on the Back Shore of Cape Cod,
where Henry Beston had gone alone
and chronicled a year spent with the elements
and the beach creatures who had no power
even to influence their portrayals in his book.
I swam, not far out; I have always felt fear
when swimming on top of very deep water.
When I came back I sat next to my mother on
      the towel,
and we ate the lunch she had wrapped in the same
CUT-RITE paper she had wrapped my sandwiches in
in J. C. Potter School, waxed to the precise degree
of cloudy translucency to indicate the extent
we saw, and the extent we did not see,
ourselves as two who had done nothing
to avert the explosion in my father's chest.
As I rubbed myself with sun oil, concentrating
in the way I concentrated on anything that
did not entail knowing what it meant
for me to be a son of him or her, she said, "Oh,
you have hair on your legs, I never thought you did."

GALWAY KINNELL   129

MY MOTHER IN OLD AGE

As my mother ages and becomes
Ever more fragile and precarious,
Her hands dwindle under her rings
And the freckled skin at her throat
Gathers in tender pleats like some startled fabric.
The blue translucence of her veins gives
The texture of her skin an agate gleam
And the dark-blue, almost indigo
Capillaries of her cheeks and forehead
Resemble the gentle roots
Of cuttings of violets
In sheltered jars.

               I love her now more urgently
Because there is an unfamiliar and relentless
Splendor in her face that terrifies me.

               "Oh, don't prettify decrepitude,"
She demands. "Don't lie!
Don't make old age seem so *ornamental!*"

And yet she abets her metamorphosis,
Invests herself in voluminous costume
Jewels and shrill polyesters

               – ambitious as a moth
To mime the dangerous leaf on which she rests.

SITTING AT NIGHT ON THE FRONT PORCH

I'm here, on the dark porch, restyled in my mother's
        chair.
10:45 and no moon.
Below the house, car lights
Swing down, on the canyon floor, to the sea.

In this they resemble us,
Dropping like match flames through the great void
Under our feet.
In this they resemble her, burning and disappearing.

Everyone's gone
And I'm here, sizing the dark, saving my mother's seat.

MY MOTHER

TO MY FIRST LOVE, MY MOTHER

Sonnets are full of love, and this my tome
Has many sonnets: so here now shall be
One sonnet more, a love sonnet, from me
To her whose heart is my heart's quiet home,
To my first Love, my Mother, on whose knee
I learnt love-lore that is not troublesome;
Whose service is my special dignity,
And she my lodestar while I go and come.
And so because you love me, and because
I love you, Mother, I have woven a wreath
Of rhymes wherewith to crown your honored name:
In you not fourscore years can dim the flame
Of love, whose blessed glow transcends the laws
Of time and change and mortal life and death.

CHRISTINA ROSSETTI   135

TO MY MOTHER

You too, my mother, read my rhymes
For love of unforgotten times,
And you may chance to hear once more
The little feet along the floor.

MOTHER'S SONG

If snow falls on the far field
where travelers
spend the night,
I ask you, cranes,
to warm my child in your wings.

MOTHER

I am always aware of my mother,
ominous, threatening,
a pain in the depths of my consciousness.
My mother is like a shell,
so easily broken.
Yet the fact that I was born
bearing my mother's shadow
cannot be changed.
She is like a cherished, bitter dream
my nerves cannot forget
even after I awake.
She prevents all freedom of movement.
If I move she quickly breaks,
and the splinters stab me.

138   NAGASE KIYOKO
     TRANSLATED BY KENNETH REXROTH
     AND IKUKO ATSUMI

MY MOTHER ONCE TOLD ME

My mother once told me
Not to sleep with flowers in the room.
Since then I have not slept with flowers.
I sleep alone, without them.

There were many flowers.
But I've never had enough time.
And persons I love are already pushing themselves
Away from my life, like boats
Away from the shore.

My mother said
Not to sleep with flowers.
You won't sleep.
You won't sleep, mother of my childhood.

The banister I clung to
When they dragged me off to school
Is long since burnt.
But my hands, clinging,
Remain
Clinging.

YEHUDA AMICHAI
TRANSLATED BY ASSIA GUTMANN

THE INTRUDER

My mother – preferring the strange to the tame:
Dove-note, bone marrow, deer dung,
Frog's belly distended with finny young,
Leaf-mould wilderness, hare-bell, toadstool,
Odd, small snakes roving through the leaves,
Metallic beetles rambling over stones: all
Wild and natural! – flashed out her instinctive love,
    and quick, she
Picked up the fluttering, bleeding bat the cat laid at
    her feet,
And held the little horror to the mirror, where
He gazed on himself, and shrieked like an old screen
    door far off.

Depended from her pinched thumb, each wing
Came clattering down like a small black shutter.
Still tranquil, she began, "It's rather sweet...."
The soft mouse body, the hard feral glint
In the caught eyes. Then we saw,
And recoiled: lice, pallid, yellow,
Nested within the wing-pits, cosily sucked and snoozed.
The thing dropped from her hands, and with its thud,
Swiftly, the cat, with a clean careful mouth
Closed on the soiled webs, growling, took them out to
    the back stoop.

But still, dark blood, a sticky puddle on the floor
Remained, of all my mother's tender, wounding
    passion
For a whole wild, lost, betrayed and secret life
Among its dens and burrows, its clean stones,
Whose denizens can turn upon the world
With spitting tongue, an odor, talon, claw,
To sting or soil benevolence, alien
As our clumsy traps, our random scatter of shot.
She swept to the kitchen. Turning on the tap,
She washed and washed the pity from her hands.

CAROLYN KIZER

MOTHER

I have a happy nature,
But Mother is always sad,
I enjoy every moment of my life, –
Mother has been had.

MA

Old photographs would have her bookish, sitting
Under a willow. I take that to be a croquet
Lawn. She reads aloud, no doubt from Rupert Brooke.
The month is always May or June.

Or with the stranger on the motor-bike.
Not my father, no. This one's all crew-cut
And polished brass buttons.
An American soldier, perhaps.
                                        And the full moon

Swaying over Keenaghan, the orchards and the cannery,
Thins to a last yellow-hammer, and goes.
The neighbours gather, all Keenaghan and Collegelands,
There is story-telling. Old miners at Coalisland
Going into the ground. Swinging, for fear of the gas,
The soft flame of a canary.

ON WALKING BACKWARDS

My mother forbad us to walk backwards. That is how
the dead walk, she would say. Where did she get this
idea? Perhaps from a bad translation. The dead, after
all, do not walk backwards but they do walk behind us.
They have no lungs and cannot call out but would love
for us to turn around. They are victims of love, many
of them.

LINES

While talking to my mother I neaten things. Spines of
    books by the phone.
Paper clips
in a china dish. Fragments of eraser that dot the desk.
    She speaks
longingly
of death. I begin tilting all the paper clips in the other
    direction.
Out
the window snow is falling straight down in lines.
    To my mother,
love
of my life, I describe what I had for brunch. The lines
    are falling
faster
now. Fate has put little weights on the ends (to speed
    us up) I
want
to tell her – sign of God's pity. She won't keep me
    (she is saying)
won't run up my bill. Miracles slip past us. The
paper clips
are immortally aligned. God's pity! How long
will
it feel like burning, said the child trying to be
kind.

ANNE CARSON   145

HANDBAG

My mother's old handbag,
crowded with letters she carried
all through the war. The smell
of my mother's handbag: mints
and lipstick and Coty powder.
The look of those letters, softened
and worn at the edges, opened,
read, and refolded so often.
Letters from my father. Odour
of leather and powder, which ever
since then has meant womanliness,
and love, and anguish, and war.

MY MOTHER ON AN EVENING IN
LATE SUMMER

When the moon appears,
and a few wind-stricken barns stand out
in the low-domed hills
and shine with a light
that is veiled and dust-filled
and that floats upon the fields,
my mother, with her hair pulled back in a bun,
her face in shadow, and the smoke
from her cigarette coiling close
to the faint yellow sheen of her dress,
stands near the house
and watches the seepage of late light
down through the sedges,
the last gray islands of cloud
taken from view, and the wind
ruffling the moon's ash-colored coat
on the black bay.

Soon the house, with its shades drawn closed,
        will send
small carpets of lampglow
into the haze and the bay
will begin its loud heaving
and the pines – frayed finials

climbing the hill – will seem to graze
the dim cinders of heaven.
And my mother will stare into the star lanes,
the endless tunnels of nothing,
and as she gazes,
under the hour's spell,
she will think how we yield each night
to the soundless storms of decay
that tear at the folding flesh,
and she will not know
why she is here
or what she is prisoner of
if not the conditions of love that brought her to this.

My mother will go indoors
and the fields, the bare stones
will drift in peace; small creatures –
the mouse and the swift – will sleep
at opposite ends of the house.
Only the cricket will be up,
repeating its one shrill note
to the rotten boards of the porch,
to the rusted screens, to the air, to the rimless dark,
to the sea that keeps to itself.
Why should my mother awake?
The earth is not yet a garden
about to be turned. The stars

are not yet bells that ring
at night for the lost.
It is much too late.

THE BLACK LACE FAN MY MOTHER
GAVE ME

It was the first gift he ever gave her,
buying it for five francs in the Galeries
in prewar Paris. It was stifling.
A starless drought made the nights stormy.

They stayed in the city for the summer.
They met in cafés. She was always early.
He was late. That evening he was later.
They wrapped the fan. He looked at his watch.

She looked down the Boulevard des Capucines.
She ordered more coffee. She stood up.
The streets were emptying. The heat was killing.
She thought the distance smelled of rain and lightning.

These are wild roses, appliquéd in silk
by hand – darkly picked, stitched boldly, quickly.
The rest is tortoiseshell and has the reticent,
clear patience of its element. It is

a worn-out, underwater bullion and it keeps,
even now, an inference of its violation.
The lace is overcast, as if the weather
it opened for and offset had entered it.

150

The past is an empty café terrace.
An airless dusk before thunder. A man running.
And no way now to know what happened then –
none at all – unless, of course, you improvise:

The blackbird on this first sultry morning
in summer, finding buds, worms, fruit,
feels the heat. Suddenly, she puts out her wing –
the whole, full, flirtatious span of it.

WHAT WE LOST

It is a winter afternoon.
The hills are frozen. Light is failing.
The distance is a crystal earshot.
A woman is mending linen in her kitchen.

She is a countrywoman.
Behind her cupboard doors she hangs sprigged,
stove-dried lavender in muslin.
Her letters and mementos and memories

are packeted in satin at the back with
gaberdine and worsted and
the cambric she has made into bodices;
the good tobacco silk for Sunday Mass.

She is sewing in the kitchen.
The sugar-feel of flax is in her hands.
Dusk. And the candles brought in then.
One by one. And the quiet sweat of wax.

There is a child at her side.
The tea is poured, the stitching put down.
The child grows still, sensing something of importance.
The woman settles and begins her story.

Believe it, what we lost is here in this room
on this veiled evening:
The woman finishes. The story ends.
The child, who is my mother, gets up, moves away.

In the winter air, unheard, unshared,
the moment happens, hangs fire, leads nowhere.
The light will fail and the room darken,
the child fall asleep and the story be forgotten.

The fields are dark already.
The frail connections have been made and are broken.
The dumb-show of legend has become language,
is becoming silence and who will know that once

words were possibilities and disappointments,
were scented closets filled with love-letters
and memories and lavender hemmed into muslin,
stored in sachets, aired in bed-linen;

and travelled silks and the tones of cotton
tautened into bodices, subtly shaped by breathing;
were the rooms of childhood with their griefless peace,
their hands and whispers, their candles weeping
        brightly?

EAVAN BOLAND   153

THE PARCEL

There are dying arts and
one of them is
the way my mother used to make up a parcel.
Paper first. Mid-brown and coarse-grained as wood.
The worst sort for covering a Latin book neatly
or laying flat at Christmas on a pudding bowl.
It was a big cylinder. She snipped it open
and it unrolled quickly across the floor.
All business, all distance.
Then the scissors.
Not a glittering let-up but a dour
pair, black thumb-holes,
the shears themselves the colour of the rained-
on steps a man with a grindstone climbed up
in the season of lilac and snapdragon
and stood there arguing the rate for
sharpening the lawnmower and the garden pair
and this one. All-in.
The ball of twine was coarsely braided
and only a shade less yellow than
the flame she held under the blunt
end of the sealing wax until
it melted and spread into a brittle
terracotta medal.
Her hair dishevelled, her tongue between her teeth,

she wrote the address in the quarters
twine had divided the surface into.
Names and places. Crayon and fountain pen.
The town underlined once. The country twice.
It's ready for the post
she would say and if we want to know
where it went to –
a craft lost before we missed it – watch it go
into the burlap sack for collection.
See it disappear. Say
this is how it died
out: among doomed steamships and outdated trains,
the tracks for them disappearing before our eyes,
next to station names we can't remember
on a continent we no longer
recognize. The sealing wax cracking.
The twine unravelling. The destination illegible.

ANNIVERSARY

My mother in her feathers of flame
Grows taller. Every May Thirteenth
I see her with her sister Miriam. I lift
The torn-off diary page where my brother jotted
"Ma died today" – and there they are.
She is now as tall as Miriam.
In the perpetual Sunday morning
Of everlasting, they are strolling together
Listening to the larks
Ringing in their orbits. The work of the cosmos,
Creation and destruction of matter
And of anti-matter
Pulses and flares, shudders and fades
Like the Northern Lights in their feathers.

My mother is telling Miriam
About her life, which was mine. Her voice comes,
    piping,
Down a deep gorge of woodland echoes:
"This is the water-line, dark on my dress, look,
Where I dragged him from the reservoir.
And that is the horse on which I galloped
Through the brick wall
And out over the heather simply
To bring him a new pen. This is the pen

I laid on the altar. And these
Are the mass marriages of him and his brother
Where I was not once a guest." Then suddenly
She is scattering the red coals with her fingers
To find where I had fallen
For the third time. She laughs
Helplessly till she weeps. Miriam
Who died at eighteen
Is Madonna-like with pure wonder
To hear of all she missed. Now my mother
Shows her the rosary prayers of unending worry,
Like pairs of shoes, or one dress after another,
"This is the sort of thing," she is saying,
"I liked to wear best." And: "Much of it,
You know, was simply sitting at the window
Watching the horizon. Truly
Wonderful it was, day after day,
Knowing they were somewhere. It still is.
Look."

And they pause, on the brink
Of the starry dew. They are looking at me.
My mother, darker with her life,
Her Red Indian hair, her skin
So strangely olive and other-worldly,

Miriam now sheer flame beside her.
Their feathers throb softly, iridescent.
My mother's face is glistening
As if she held it into the skyline wind
Looking towards me. I do this for her.

She is using me to tune finer
Her weeping love for my brother, through mine,
As if I were the shadow cast by his approach.

As when I came a mile over fields and walls
Towards her, and found her weeping for him –
Able for all that distance to think me him.

I ASK MY MOTHER TO SING

She begins, and my grandmother joins her.
Mother and daughter sing like young girls.
If my father were alive, he would play
his accordion and sway like a boat.

I've never been in Peking, or the Summer Palace,
nor stood on the great Stone Boat to watch
the rain begin on Kuen Ming Lake, the picnickers
running away in the grass.

But I love to hear it sung;
how the waterlilies fill with rain until
they overturn, spilling water into water,
then rock back, and fill with more.

Both women have begun to cry.
But neither stops her song.

MOTHERS
for J.B.

Oh mother,
here in your lap,
as good as a bowlful of clouds,
I your greedy child
am given your breast,
the sea wrapped in skin,
and your arms,
roots covered with moss
and with new shoots sticking out
to tickle the laugh out of me.
Yes, I am wedded to my teddy
but he has the smell of you
as well as the smell of me.
Your necklace that I finger
is all angel eyes.
Your rings that sparkle
are like the moon on the pond.
Your legs that bounce me up and down,
your dear nylon-covered legs,
are the horses I will ride
into eternity.

Oh mother,
after this lap of childhood
I will never go forth
into the big people's world
as an alien,
a fabrication,
or falter
when someone else
is as empty as a shoe.

IN AN IRIDESCENT TIME

My mother, when young, scrubbed laundry in a tub,
She and her sisters on an old brick walk
Under the apple trees, sweet rub-a-dub.
The bees came round their heads, and wrens made talk.
Four young ladies each with a rainbow board
Honed their knuckles, wrung their wrists to red,
Tossed back their braids and wiped their aprons wet.
The Jersey calf beyond the back fence roared;
And all the soft day, swarms about their pet
Buzzed at his big brown eyes and bullish head.
Four times they rinsed, they said. Some things they
      starched,
Then shook them from the baskets two by two,
And pinned the fluttering intimacies of life
Between the lilac bushes and the yew:
Brown gingham, pink, and skirts of Alice blue.

MY MOTHER

My mother comes back from a trip downtown to the dime store. She has brought me a surprise. It is still in her purse.

She is wearing her red shoes with straps across the instep. They fasten with small white buttons, like the eyes of fish.

She brings back zippers and spools of thread, yellow and green, for her work, which always takes her far away, even though she works upstairs, in the room next to mine.

She is wearing her blue plaid full-skirted dress with the large collar, her hair fastened up off her neck. She looks pretty. She always dresses up when she goes downtown.

Now she opens her straw purse, which looks like a small suitcase. She hands me the new toy: a wooden paddle with a red rubber ball attached to it by an elastic string. Sometimes when she goes downtown, I think she will not come back.

MY GRANDMOTHER

AMONG WOMEN

What women wander?
Not many. All. A few.
Most would, now & then,
& no wonder.
Some, and I'm one,

Wander sitting still.
My small grandmother
Bought from every peddler
Less for the ribbons and lace
Than for their scent
Of sleep where you will,
Walk out when you want, choose
Your bread and your company.

She warned me, "Have nothing to lose."

She looked fragile but had
High blood, runner's ankles,
Could endure, endure.
She loved her rooted garden, her
Grand children, her once
Wild once young man.
Women wander
As best they can.

MARIE PONSOT   167

GRANDMOTHER WATCHING AT HER WINDOW

There was always the river or the train
Right past the door, and someone might be gone
Come morning. When I was a child I mind
Being held up at a gate to wave
Good-bye, good-bye to I didn't know who,
Gone to the War, and how I cried after.
When I married I did what was right
But I knew even that first night
That he would go. And so shut my soul tight
Behind my mouth, so he could not steal it
When he went. I brought the children up clean
With my needle, taught them that stealing
Is the worst sin; knew if I loved them
They would be taken away, and did my best
But must have loved them anyway
For they slipped through my fingers like stitches.
Because God loves us always, whatever
We do. You can sit all your life in churches
And teach your hands to clutch when you pray
And never weaken, but God loves you so dearly
Just as you are, that nothing you are can stay,
But all the time you keep going away, away.

LINEAGE

My grandmothers were strong.
They followed plows and bent to toil.
They moved through fields sowing seed.
They touched earth and grain grew.
They were full of sturdiness and singing.
My grandmothers were strong.
My grandmothers are full of memories
Smelling of soap and onions and wet clay
With veins rolling roughly over quick hands
They have many clean words to say.
My grandmothers were strong.
Why am I not as they?

LEGACIES

her grandmother called her from the playground
    "yes, ma'am" said the little girl
    "i want chu to learn how to make rolls" said the old
woman proudly
but the little girl didn't want
to learn how because she knew
even if she couldn't say it that
that would mean when the old one died she would
    be less
dependent on her spirit so
the little girl said
    "i don't want to know how to make no rolls"
with her lips poked out
and the old woman wiped her hands on
her apron saying "lord
    these children"
and neither of them ever
said what they meant
and i guess nobody ever does

GETTING READY FOR THE NIGHT

When Grandma combed her fine white hair at night
until it toppled to her shoulder blades
in startling cascades, bright-angel-winged,
she looked like Milton's seraph at the gate
of Paradise: sovereign, ingenuous, and stern.
I marvelled in the ripples of her hair
the teasing and impertinent lamplight touched,
but "Won't you clip my toenails for me now?"
she said, and then, with a stoic sigh,
"It's hard to be so old, so incapable."
I didn't want to touch her pallid foot
and yet it felt astonishing when her left
foot nestled in my clasp and I began
scissoring the wrinkled horn of nail
with snipping shears until the pale
translucencies of toenail ribboned off.
Her sole felt warm in my deft paw
and suddenly I could appreciate
Grandma being mortal, one who sheds
skin and nails and all integuments . . .

But then she twined
and spooled her colorless flat hair
about accustomed fingers into supple
braids

and I was baffled in the tenderness
her silk-shaded light winked down on both of us.

                    I snipped her toenails
evenly. Together we prepared her
for the night. Together we made sure
that, shorn and braided, she would enter into
the encirclements of darkness just beyond
the pooled, penurious empire
of the lamp.

MY GRANDMOTHER IS WAITING FOR
ME TO COME HOME

My Grandmother is waiting for me to come home.
We live with walnuts and apples
in a one-room kitchenette above The
Some Day Liquor Gardens.

My Grandmother sits in a red rocking chair
waiting for me
to open the door with my key.

She is Black and glossy like coal.

We eat walnuts and apples,
drink root beer in cups that are broken,
above The
Some Day Liquor Gardens.

I love my Grandmother.
She is wonderful to behold
with the glossy of her coal-colored skin.
She is warm wide and long.
She laughs and she Lingers.

THE NEEDLE

Grandmother, you are as pale
as Christ's hands on the wall above you.
When you close your eyes you are all
white – hair, skin, gown. I blink
to find you again in the bed.

I remember once you told me
you weighed a hundred and twenty-three,
the day you married Grandfather.
You had handsome legs. He watched you
working at the sink.

The soft ring is loose on your hand.
I hated coming here.
I know you can't understand me.
I'll try again,
like the young nurse with the needle.

IRONING GRANDMOTHER'S TABLECLOTH

As a bride, you made it smooth,
pulling the edges straight, the corners square.
For years you went over the same piece
of cloth, the way Grandfather walked to work.

This morning I move the iron across the damask,
back and forth, up and down. You are ninety-four.
Each day you dress yourself, then go back to bed
and listen to radio sermons, staring at the ceiling.

When I visit, you tell me your troubles:
how my father left poisoned grapefruit on the back
porch at Christmas, how somebody comes at night
to throw stones at the house.

The streets of your brain become smaller,
old houses torn down. Talking to me
is hard work, keeping things straight,
whose child I am, whether I have children.

CHURCH FAIR

Who knows what I might find
on tables under the maple trees –
perhaps a saucer in Aunt Lois's china pattern
to replace the one I broke
the summer I was thirteen, and visiting
for a week. Never in all these years
have I thought of it without
a warm surge of embarrassment.

I'll go through my own closets and cupboards
to find things for the auction.
I'll bake a peach pie for the food table,
and rolls for the supper,
Grandma Kenyon's recipe, which came down to me
along with her sturdy legs and brooding disposition.
"Mrs. Kenyon," the doctor used to tell her,
"you are simply killing yourself with work."
This she repeated often, with keen satisfaction.

She lived to be a hundred and three,
surviving all her children,
including the one so sickly at birth
that she had to carry him everywhere on a pillow
for the first four months. Father
suffered from a weak chest – bronchitis,

176

pneumonias, and pleurisy – and early on
books and music became his joy.

Surely these clothes are from another life –
not my own. I'll drop them off on the way
to town. I'm getting the peaches
today, so they'll be ripe by Saturday.

ADAGES OF A GRANDMOTHER

Grandmother said to me, "Keep thyself
unspotted from the world." She spoke in quotes.
I got the feeling that she had rehearsed
all her admonitions as a child,
for when she issued them to me she grew
solemn and theatrical. I knew
she tasted in her words some sweet,
indissoluble flavor of the past; but even more,
as though at eighty-five or eighty-six
she stood still in the parlor of her recitation –
a plain, studious girl with long, brown braids
(I have the portraits of her as a child) –
and spoke her lessons for approving guests.
Such touches of girlishness accompanied
her adages. And then she gave me dimes
for so many lines of Shakespeare memorized.
For "The quality of mercy..." I was paid
a quarter, and at tea I gave her guests
a dollar's worth of Shakespeare with their toast.
"All the world's a stage," she reminded me.

Only armed with an adage might I sally forth.
"A foolish son's his mother's grief," she thought.
The world was scriptural and stratified.
It held raw veins of wisdom in its side,

like the Appalachians when we journeyed north.
She sat in the front seat of the Buick, hairnet drawn
over her white hair coiled in a dignified bun,
her straw, beflowered hat alert and prim.
From the back seat I'd study her, my grim
grandmother, with her dictatorial
chin, her gold-rimmed spectacles ablaze with all
the glory of the common highway where
field daisies spoke to her in doctrinaire
confidential accents of the master plan
confided to grandmothers by the Son of Man.
Wisdom was talismanic and opaque –
could be carried in a child's small fist
like the personal pebble I fished out of the lake.
And whenever I stepped outside she kissed
my head and armed me with a similitude.
Beyond the screen door, past the windowsill,
the bright earth rang with providence until
even the wise ants at my shoe tips moved
in dark amazements of exactitude,
and the small dusty sparrows swooped innumerably.

I write this on the sun porch of the house
where she lay, an invalid, in her last years.
And I'm abashed to realize I blamed

her stiffness and her stubborn uprightness
for much that happened to me afterward.
Now I look through the window where she looked
and see the sunlight on the windowsill
and wonder what it signifies,
for now I barely recognize
her world outside, as though sunlight effaced
not only human features but their memory.
Her adages are all scattered in my head
(*Neither a borrower, nor a lender be*),
and I cannot think for thinking of the dead
(*Go to the ant, thou sluggard;*
consider her ways, and be wise);
I cannot read the world now with her eyes
(*Sit, Jessica. Look how the floor of heaven*
is thick inlaid with patines of bright gold).
And I, who used to blame her so,
rummage in my pockets for
a nickel's worth of wisdom for my kids.

From GRANDMOTHERS

1. *Mary Gravely Jones*
We had no petnames, no diminutives for you,
always the formal guest under my father's roof:
you were "Grandmother Jones" and you visited rarely.
I see you walking up and down the garden,
restless, southern-accented, reserved, you did not seem
my mother's mother or anyone's grandmother.
You were Mary, widow of William, and no matriarch,
yet smoldering to the end with frustrate life,
ideas nobody listened to, least of all my father.
One summer night you sat with my sister and me
in the wooden glider long after twilight,
holding us there with streams of pent-up words.
You could quote every poet I had ever heard of,
had read *The Opium Eater*, Amiel and Bernard Shaw,
your green eyes looked clenched against opposition.
You married straight out of the convent school,
your background was country, you left an unperformed
typescript of a play about Burr and Hamilton,
you were impotent and brilliant, no one cared
about your mind, you might have ended
elsewhere than in that glider
reciting your unwritten novels to the children.

2. Hattie Rice Rich

Your sweetness of soul was a mystery to me,
you who slip-covered chairs, glued broken china,
lived out of a wardrobe trunk in our guestroom
summer and fall, then took the Pullman train
in your darkblue dress and straw hat, to Alabama,
shuttling half-yearly between your son and daughter.
Your sweetness of soul was a convenience for everyone,
how you rose with the birds and children, boiled your
      own egg,
fished for hours on a pier, your umbrella spread,
took the street-car downtown shopping
endlessly for your son's whims, the whims of genius,
kept your accounts in ledgers, wrote letters daily.
All through World War Two the forbidden word
Jewish was barely uttered in your son's house;
your anger flared over inscrutable things.
Once I saw you crouched on the guestroom bed,
knuckles blue-white around the bedpost, sobbing
your one brief memorable scene of rebellion:
you didn't want to go back South that year.
You were never "Grandmother Rich" but "Anana";
you had money of your own but you were homeless,
Hattie, widow of Samuel, and no matriarch,
dispersed among the children and grandchildren.

MY GRANDMOTHER'S
LOVE LETTERS

There are no stars to-night
But those of memory.
Yet how much room for memory there is
In the loose girdle of soft rain.

There is even room enough
For the letters of my mother's mother,
Elizabeth,
That have been pressed so long
Into a corner of the roof
That they are brown and soft,
And liable to melt as snow.

Over the greatness of such space
Steps must be gentle.
It is all hung by an invisible white hair.
It trembles as birch limbs webbing the air.

And I ask myself:

"Are your fingers long enough to play
Old keys that are but echoes:
Is the silence strong enough
To carry back the music to its source
And back to you again
As though to her?"

Yet I would lead my grandmother by the hand
Through much of what she would not understand;
And so I stumble. And the rain continues on the roof
With such a sound of gently pitying laughter.

SESTINA

September rain falls on the house.
In the failing light, the old grandmother
sits in the kitchen with the child
beside the Little Marvel Stove,
reading the jokes from the almanac,
laughing and talking to hide her tears.

She thinks that her equinoctial tears
and the rain that beats on the roof of the house
were both foretold by the almanac,
but only known to a grandmother.
The iron kettle sings on the stove.
She cuts some bread and says to the child,

It's time for tea now; but the child
is watching the teakettle's small hard tears
dance like mad on the hot black stove,
the way the rain must dance on the house.
Tidying up, the old grandmother
hangs up the clever almanac

on its string. Birdlike, the almanac
hovers half open above the child,
hovers above the old grandmother
and her teacup full of dark brown tears.

She shivers and says she thinks the house
feels chilly, and puts more wood in the stove.

It was to be, says the Marvel Stove.
I know what I know, says the almanac.
With crayons the child draws a rigid house
and a winding pathway. Then the child
puts in a man with buttons like tears
and shows it proudly to the grandmother.

But secretly, while the grandmother
busies herself about the stove,
the little moons fall down like tears
from between the pages of the almanac
into the flower bed the child
has carefully placed in the front of the house.

Time to plant tears, says the almanac.
The grandmother sings to the marvellous stove
and the child draws another inscrutable house.

ABSENCE AND LOSS

AFTER THE DEATH OF HER
DAUGHTER IN CHILDBIRTH,
LOOKING AT THE CHILD

Leaving us behind,
Whom will she have pitied more –
Infant or mother?
My child it was for me:
Her child it must have been.

Recklessly
I cast myself away;
Perhaps
A heart in love
Becomes a deep ravine?

Never could I think
Our love a worldly commonplace
On this morning when
For the first time my heart
Is filled with many thoughts.

As the rains of spring
Fall, day after day, so I
Fare on through time
While by the fence the grasses grow
And green spreads everywhere.

From that first night,
Although I have not wept
Cold, rainy tears upon my bed,
Yet I have recklessly
Slept in strange places and strange ways.

From darkness
Into the path of darkness
Must I enter:
Shine upon me from afar,
O moon above the mountain crest.

TRANSLATED BY EDWIN A. CRANSTON

TO AN ABSENT DAUGHTER

Where art thou, bird of song?
Brightest one and dearest?
Other groves among,
Other nests thou cheerest;
Sweet thy warbling skill
To each ear that heard thee,
But 'twas sweetest still
To the heart that rear'd thee.

Lamb, where dost thou rest?
On stranger-bosoms lying?
Flowers, thy path that drest,
All uncropp'd are dying;
Streams where thou didst roam
Murmur on without thee,
Lov'st thou still thy home?
Can thy mother doubt thee?

Seek thy Saviour, flock,
To his blest fold going,
Seek that smitten rock
Whence our peace is flowing;
Still should Love rejoice,
Whatsoe'er betide thee,
If that Shepherd's voice
Evermore might guide thee.

LYDIA HUNTLEY SIGOURNEY   191

MATERNITY

One wept whose only child was dead,
New-born, ten years ago.
"Weep not; he is in bliss," they said.
She answered, "Even so,

"Ten years ago was born in pain
A child, not now forlorn.
But oh, ten years ago, in vain,
A mother, a mother was born."

ON MY BOY HENRY

Here lies a boy, the finest child from me,
Which makes my heart and soul sigh for to see,
Nor can I think of any thought, but grieve,
For joy or pleasure could me not relieve;
It lived days as many as my years,
No more, which caused my grievéd tears;
Twenty and nine was the number,
And death hath parted us asunder;
But you are happy, sweetest, on high,
I mourn not for thy birth, nor cry.

LADY ELIZABETH EGERTON,   193
COUNTESS OF BRIDGEWATER

THE MOTHER'S CHARGE

She raised her head. With hot and glittering eye,
"I know," she said, "that I am going to die.
Come here, my daughter, while my mind is clear.
Let me make plain to you your duty here;
My duty once – I never failed to try –
But for some reason I am going to die."
She raised her head, and, while her eyes rolled wild,
Poured these instructions on the gasping child:
"Begin at once – don't iron sitting down –
Wash your potatoes when the fat is brown –
Monday, unless it rains – it always pays
To get fall sewing done on the right days –
A carpet-sweeper and a little broom –
Save dishes – wash the summer dining room
With soda – keep the children out of doors –
The starch is out – beeswax on all the floors –
If girls are treated like your friends they stay –
They stay, and treat you like their friends – the way
To make home happy is to keep a jar –
And save the prettiest pieces for the star
In the middle – blue's too dark – all silk is best –
And don't forget the corners – when they're dressed
Put them on ice – and always wash the chest
Three times a day, the windows every week –
We need more flour – the bedroom ceilings leak –

It's better than onion – keep the boys at home –
Gardening is good – a load, three loads of loam –
They bloom in spring – and smile, smile always, dear –
Be brave, keep on – I hope I've made it clear."
She died, as all her mothers died before.
Her daughter died in turn, and made one more.

HEIRLOOM

Among a few small objects I've taken from my
mother's house is this heavy, hand-size, cut-glass
saltcellar, cheap and solid, its facets speaking her at
the dining-room table reaching for the salt or passing
it to my father at the far end, his back to the window.
The table is a time bomb, ticking in the play of light
on the white cloth, a current of electric silence that
holds us all in our blind clutching after straws of talk,
Father hidden behind the newspaper, Mother filling
our plates with food, my tongue blunted between
them, the way they couldn't meet each other's eyes,
the tablecloth a snowfield they couldn't cross to rescue
one another before the next fall wiped everything
away again, taking the faint traces their feet had made
once dancing. He'd leave the table early for an
armchair, *just a glance at the evening paper*, and she'd sit
on until – all small talk exhausted – we'd clear the
table, stack dirty dishes by the sink in the scullery,
storing the saltcellar in the press, where it would
absorb small tears of air until the next time we'd need
its necessary, bitter addition, as now it stands on our
kitchen table over here and is carried to the dining
room for meals, a solid object filling my hand, a
presence at the center of our talk, its cut glass
outlasting flesh and blood as heirlooms do. I take its

salt to the tip of my tongue, testing its savor and
spilling by chance a tiny white hieroglyph of grains,
which I pinch in my mother's superstitious fingers and
quickly scatter over my own left shoulder, keeping at
bay and safe the darker shades.

THE WAKE
(*Pollsmoor Prison, 1978*)

when my mother was dying
I had to flay my way through the seething current
to reach the bedstead where they had laid her out
in the yard: sparkling yellow
the sun stroked the Arcadian scene
playing up the choir of ancient faces of extinct
uncles and forefathers sitting peacefully
sucking pipes to warble smoke,

strong and chipper she was under the white sheet
her eyes luminous and somewhat surprised without
      the spectacles
her plumpish arms distributing with deliberate gestures
the ultimate messages and blessings
(only the tired gray bun had already come undone):
visions of everything going swimmingly and she
at rest now with inter alia Matthew and Mark left and
right the two old geezers were by Jove standing to,

and she also kept on beckoning me by name
and could not place me at all,

but I had to retrace my steps lest the authorities
get wind of my escape into the current's

198

quickening whirl I sank
(was this the great drowning?)
to wash up teeth a-chatter lower down between banks
somewhere past farmlands where mud-spattered
grain elevators slash the heavens where haystacks
rot and turnips are gorged down by the turf,

and straining at their leashes I heard the stinking
dogs their throats clogged with the yelping fury of
      the hunt

BREYTEN BREYTENBACH
TRANSLATED, FROM THE AFRIKAANS,
BY THE AUTHOR

UPON THE SIGHT OF MY ABORTIVE BIRTH THE 31ST OF DECEMBER 1657

What birth is this, a poor despiséd creature?
  A little embryo, void of life, and feature.

Seven times I went my time, when mercy giving
  deliverance unto me and mine, all living,

Strong, right proportioned, lovely girls and boys,
  Their father's, mother's present, hoped-for joys.

That was great wisdom, goodness, power, love, praise
  to my dear Lord, lovely in all his ways.

This is no less. The same God hath it done.
  Submits my heart: that's better than a son.

In giving, taking, stroking, striking, still
  His glory and my good is His my will

In that then, this now, both, good God most mild.
  His will's more dear to me than any child.

I also joy, that God hath gained one more
  To praise him in the heavens than was before,

And that this babe, as well as all the rest,
   since it had a soul, shall be for ever blest.

That I'm made instrumental to both these –
   God's praise, babes' bliss – it highly doth me please.

Maybe the Lord looks for more thankfulness
   and high esteem for those I do possess.

As limners draw dead shades for to set forth
   their lively colours and their pictures' worth,

So doth my God, in this as all things wise,
   By my dead formless babe teach me to prize

My living pretty pair, Nat and Bethia,
   the children dear God yet lends to Maria.

Praised be His name. This two's full compensation
   For all that's gone and that in expectation,

And if herein God hath fulfilled His will,
   His hand-maid's pleased, completely happy still.

I only now desire of my sweet God
   the reason why He took in hand His rod.

What He doth spy? what is the thing amiss?
   I fain would learn, whilst I the rod do kiss.

Methinks I hear God's voice: "This is thy sin,"
   (And conscience justifies the same within)

"Thou often dost present me with dead fruit.
   Why should not my returns, thy presents suit?

"Dead duties, prayers, praises, thou dost bring,
   affections dead, dead heart in everything,

"In hearing, reading, conference, meditation,
   in acting, graces and in conversation.

"Who's taught or bettered by you? No relation.
   Thou art cause of mourning, not of imitation.

"Thou dost not answer that great means I give.
   My word, and ordinances do teach to live.

"Lively, oh, do it." Thy mercies are most sweet,
   Chastisements sharp and all the means that's meet.

"Mend now my child, and lively fruit bring me,
  so thou advantaged much by this wilt be."

My dearest Lord, Thy charge and more is true.
  I see it, am humbled, and for pardon sue.

In Christ forgive and henceforth I will be –
  "What?" Nothing, Lord: but what Thou makest me.

I am nought, have nought, can do nothing but sin,
  as my experience saith, for I've been in

Several conditions, trials great and many.
  In all I find my nothingness; not any-

Thing do I own but sin. Christ is my all,
  that I do want, can crave; or ever shall.

That good that suiteth all my whole desires
  and for me unto God, all he requires,

It is in Christ. He's mine, and I am His.
  This union is my only happiness;

But, Lord, since I'm a child by mercy free,
  Let me by filial fruits much honour Thee.

I'm a branch of the vine. Purge me therefore,
    Father, more fruit to bring than heretofore.

A plant in God's house, Oh! that I may be,
    more flourishing in age, a growing tree.

Let not my heart, as doth my womb, miscarry,
    but, precious means received, let it tarry

Till it be formed of gospel's shape and suit,
    my means, my mercies, and be pleasant fruit.

In my whole life, lively do thou make me.
    For Thy praise and name's sake, Oh, quicken me!

Lord, I beg quickening grace. That grace afford!
    Quicken me, Lord, according to Thy Word.

It is a lovely boon I make to Thee.
    After Thy loving kindness, quicken me.

Thy quickening spirit unto me convey;
    and thereby quicken me, in Thine own way.

And let the presence of Thy spirit dear
    be witnessed by His fruits. Let them appear

To, for Thee: love, joy, peace, gentleness,
    long-suffering, goodness, faith and much meekness.

And let my walking in the Spirit say,
    I live in it and desire it to obey,

And since my heart Thou'st lifted up to Thee,
    amend it, Lord and keep it still with Thee.

Saith Maria Carey
always in Christ happy.

THE MOTHER

Abortions will not let you forget.
You remember the children you got that you did
     not get,
The damp small pulps with a little or with no hair,
The singers and workers that never handled the air.
You will never neglect or beat
Them, or silence or buy with a sweet.
You will never wind up the sucking-thumb
Or scuttle off ghosts that come.
You will never leave them, controlling your
     luscious sigh,
Return for a snack of them, with gobbling mother-eye.

I have heard in the voices of the wind the voices of my
     dim killed children.
I have contracted. I have eased
My dim dears at the breasts they could never suck.
I have said, Sweets, if I sinned, if I seized
Your luck
And your lives from your unfinished reach,
If I stole your births and your names,
Your straight baby tears and your games,
Your stilted or lovely loves, your tumults, your
     marriages, aches, and your deaths,
If I poisoned the beginnings of your breaths,

Believe that even in my deliberateness I was not
     deliberate.
Though why should I whine,
Whine that the crime was other than mine? –
Since anyhow you are dead.
Or rather, or instead,
You were never made.
But that too, I am afraid,
Is faulty: oh, what shall I say, how is the truth to
     be said?
You were born, you had body, you died.
It is just that you never giggled or planned or cried.

Believe me, I loved you all.
Believe me, I knew you, though faintly, and I loved,
     I loved you
All.

ON VISITING THE GRAVE OF MY STILLBORN LITTLE GIRL
Sunday July 4th 1836

I made a vow within my soul, O Child,
When thou wert laid beside my weary heart,
With marks of death on every tender part
That, if in time a living infant smiled,
Winning my ear with gentle sounds of love
In sunshine of such joy, I still would save
A green rest for thy memory, O Dove!
And oft times visit thy small, nameless grave.
Thee have I not forgot, my firstborn, though
Whose eyes ne'er opened to my wistful gaze,
Whose sufferings stamped with pain thy little brow;
I think of thee in these far happier days,
And thou, my child, from thy bright heaven see
How well I keep my faithful vow to thee.

DIALOGUE

If an angel came with one wish
I might say, deliver that child
who died before birth, into life.
Let me see what she might have become.
He would bring her into a room
fair skinned   the bones of her hands
would press on my shoulderblades
in our long embrace

                        we would sit
with the albums spread on our knees:
now here are your brothers   and here
your sister   here the old house
among trees and espaliered almonds.
– But where am I?

                     Ah my dear
I have only one picture

                    here
in my head   I saw you lying
still folded   one moment   forever
your head bent down to your heart
eyes closed on unspeakable wisdom
your delicate frog-pale fingers

                        spread
apart as if you were playing
a woodwind instrument.

– My name?

                    It was never given.

– Where is my grave?

                 in my head   I suppose
the hospital burnt you.

– Was I beautiful?

               To me.

– Do you mourn for me every day?

Not at all   it is more than thirty years
I am feeling the coolness of age
the perspectives of memory change.
Pearlskull   what lifts you here
from night-drift to solemn ripeness?
Mushroom dome? Gourd plumpness?
The frog in my pot of basil?

    – It is none of these, but a rhythm
      the bones of my fingers   dactylic
      rhetoric smashed from your memory.
      Forget me again.

                  Had I lived
    no rhythm would be the same
    nor my brothers and sister feast
    in the world's eternal house.

Overhead   wings of cloud
     burning   and under my feet
         stones marked with demons' teeth.

A MOTHER IN A REFUGEE CAMP

No Madonna and Child could touch
Her tenderness for a son
She soon would have to forget....
The air was heavy with odors of diarrhea,
Of unwashed children with washed-out ribs
And dried-up bottoms waddling in labored steps
Behind blown-empty bellies. Other mothers there
Had long ceased to care, but not this one:
She held a ghost-smile between her teeth,
And in her eyes the memory
Of a mother's pride.... She had bathed him
And rubbed him down with bare palms.
She took from their bundle of possessions
A broken comb and combed
The rust-colored hair left on his skull
And then – humming in her eyes – began carefully to
    part it.
In their former life this was perhaps
A little daily act of no consequence
Before his breakfast and school; now she did it
Like putting flowers on a tiny grave.

LOVE

Dark falls on this Midwestern town
where we once lived when myths collided.
Dusk has hidden the bridge in the river
which slides and deepens
to become the water
the hero passed on his way to Hell.
Not far from here is our old apartment.
We had a kitchen and an Amish table.
We had a view. And we discovered there
love had the feather and muscle of wings
and had come to live with us,
a brother of fire and air.

We had two infant children, one of whom
was touched by death in this town
and spared: and when the hero
was hailed by his comrades in Hell
their mouths opened and their voices failed and
there is no knowing what they would have asked
about a life they had shared and lost.

I am your wife.
It was years ago.
Our child is healed. We love each other still.
Across our day-to-day and ordinary distances
we speak plainly. We hear each other clearly.

And yet I want to return to you
on the bridge of the Iowa river where you were,
with snow on the shoulders of your coat
and a car passing with its headlights on:
I see you as a hero in a text –
the image blazing and the edges gilded –
and I long to cry out the epic question,
my dear companion:
Will we ever live so intensely again?
Will love come to us again and be
so formidable at rest it offered us ascension
even to look at him?
But the words are shadows and you cannot hear me.
You walk away and I cannot follow.

IN MEMORY OF MY MOTHER

I do not think of you lying in the wet clay
Of a Monaghan graveyard; I see
You walking down a lane among the poplars
On your way to the station, or happily

Going to second Mass on a summer Sunday –
You meet me and you say:
"Don't forget to see about the cattle –"
Among your earthiest words the angels stray.

And I think of you walking along a headland
Of green oats in June,
So full of purpose, so rich with life –
And I see us meeting at the end of a town

On a fair day by accident, after
The bargains are all made and we can walk
Together through the shops and stalls and markets
Free in the oriental streets of thought.

O you are not lying in the wet clay,
For it is a harvest evening now and we
Are piling up the ricks against the moonlight
And you smile up at us – eternally.

CHILDHOOD HOUSE

After our mother died, her house, our
childhood house, disclosed
all its deterioration to our eyes.
While living she had screened us from, or we
        hadn't seen,
the termite-nibbled floorboards and the rotting beams;
the wounded stucco hidden by shrubbery; the frayed,
unpredictable wiring, and the clanking labor
of the hot-water line into the discolored
tub; the fixtures in the dining room
skewed and malfunctioning.

                        I remember thinking with a
swarm of confusion that this was the true state
of our childhood now: this house of dilapidated girders
eaten away at the base. Somehow I had assumed
that the past stood still, in perfected effigies of itself,
and that what we had once possessed remained our
        possession
forever, and that at least the past, our past, our child-
hood, waited, always available, at the touch of a nerve,
did not deteriorate like the untended house of an
aging mother, but stood in pristine perfection, as in
our remembrance. I see that this isn't so, that
memory decays like the rest, is unstable in its essence,

flits, occludes, is variable, sidesteps, bleeds away, eludes
all recovery; worse, is not what it seemed once, alters
unfairly, is not the intact garden we remember but,
instead, speeds away from us backward terrifically
until when we pause to touch that sun-remembered
wall the stones are friable, crack and sift down,
and we could cry at the fierceness of that velocity
if our astonished eyes had time.

NOT DYING

These wrinkles are nothing.
These gray hairs are nothing.
This stomach which sags
with old food, these bruised
and swollen ankles,
my darkening brain,
they are nothing.
I am the same boy
my mother used to kiss.

The years change nothing.
On windless summer nights
I feel those kisses
slide from her dark
lips far away,
and in winter they float
over the frozen pines
and arrive covered with snow.
They keep me young.

My passion for milk
is uncontrollable still.
I am driven by innocence.
From bed to chair I crawl
and back again.

I shall not die.
The grave result
and token of birth, my body
remembers and holds fast.

AFTER THE PASTORAL

Just after dusk the tulips still show yellow.

This year my child goes where I can't follow.
My first is gone, the one where I began.
"Come back," I whisper. "Come in if you can."
Silence. I step out, ferocious with fear.
Dread enters my one, trance my other, ear.
The tulips fade. I drowse until dawn breaks.
My eyes open. I force myself awake.
Cowbirds crowd the ground wherever I look.

Where soft mouths taste the night, it sets its hook.

SONG OF AMARGO'S MOTHER

They carry him on my bed sheet,
my oleanders and my palm.

The twenty-seventh day of August
with a little knife of gold.

The cross, and that was that!
He was brown and bitter.

Neighbors, give me a brass
pitcher with lemonade.

The cross. Don't anyone cry.
Amargo is on the moon.

FEDERICO GARCÍA LORCA
TRANSLATED BY JEROME ROTHENBERG

MY MOTHER'S R & R

She lay late in bed. Maybe she was sick,
though she was never sick. Pink flowers
were in full blossom in the wallpaper
and motes like bits of something ground up
churned in sunrays from the windows.
We climbed into bed with her.
Perhaps she needed comforting,
and she was alone, and she let us take
a breast each out of the loose slip.
"Let's make believe we're babies,"
Derry said. We put the large pink
flowers at the end of those lax breasts
into our mouths and sucked with enthusiasm.
She laughed and seemed to enjoy our play.
Perhaps intoxicated by our pleasure,
or frustrated by the failure of the milk
to flow, we sucked harder, probably
our bodies writhed, our eyes flared,
certainly she could feel our teeth.
Abruptly she took back her breasts
and sent us from the bed, two small
hungry boys enflamed and driven off
by the she-wolf. But we had got our nip,
and in the empire we would found,
we would taste all the women and expel them
one after another as they came to resemble her.

GOODBYE

1

My mother, poor woman, lies tonight
in her last bed. It's snowing, for her, in her darkness.
I swallow down the goodbyes I won't ever get to use,
tasteless, with wretched mouth-water;
whatever we are, she and I, we're nearly cured.

The night years ago when I walked away
from that final class of junior high school students
in Pittsburgh, the youngest of them chased
after me down the dark street. "Goodbye!" she called,
snow swirling across her face, tears shining.

2

Tears have a history of falling. Gravity
has taught them a topographical understanding
of the human face. At each last embrace
the snow brings down its ragged curtain.
The mind shreds the present, once the past is over.

In the Derry graveyard where only her longings sleep
and armfuls of flowers go out in the drizzle,
the bodies not yet risen must lie nearly forever.
"Sprouting good Irish grass," the graveskeeper blarneys,
he can't help it, "a sprig of shamrock, if they were young."

3

In Pittsburgh tonight, those who were young
will be less young, those who were old, more old,
    or likely
no more; and the street where Syllest,
fleetest of my darlings, caught up with me
and hugged me and said goodbye will be empty. Well,

one day the streets all over the world will be empty –
already in heaven the golden cobblestones have
    fallen still –
everyone's arms will be empty, everyone's mouth, the
    Derry earth.
It is written in our hearts, the emptiness is all.
That is how we have learned, the embrace is all.

From KADDISH
For Naomi Ginsberg 1894–1956

O mother
what have I left out
O mother
what have I forgotten
O mother
farewell
with a long black shoe
farewell
with Communist Party and a broken stocking
farewell
with six dark hairs on the wen of your breast
farewell
with your old dress and a long black beard around
    the vagina
farewell
with your sagging belly
with your fear of Hitler
with your mouth of bad short stories
with your fingers of rotten mandolines
with your arms of fat Paterson porches
with your belly of strikes and smokestacks
with your chin of Trotsky and the Spanish War
with your voice singing for the decaying overbroken
    workers

with your nose of bad lay with your nose of the smell
     of the pickles of Newark
with your eyes
with your eyes of Russia
with your eyes of no money
with your eyes of false China
with your eyes of Aunt Elanor
with your eyes of starving India
with your eyes pissing in the park
with your eyes of America taking a fall
with your eyes of your failure at the piano
with your eyes of your relatives in California
with your eyes of Ma Rainey dying in an ambulance
with your eyes of Czechoslovakia attacked by robots
with your eyes going to painting class at night in the
     Bronx
with your eyes of the killer Grandma you see on the
     horizon from the Fire-Escape
with your eyes running naked out of the apartment
     screaming into the hall
with your eyes being led away by policemen to an
     ambulance
with your eyes strapped down on the operating table
with your eyes with the pancreas removed

with your eyes of appendix operation
with your eyes of abortion
with your eyes of ovaries removed
with your eyes of shock
with your eyes of lobotomy
with your eyes of divorce
with your eyes of stroke
with your eyes alone
with your eyes
with your eyes
with your Death full of Flowers

MISCARRIAGE

The womb refused,
backed up,
its particles of silk
wasted, perish.
Breathless –
the cloudy silo,
the yolk sea.

In the ceremony
of lifting
and enclosing
the womb refused.
The ceremony of no-child
followed.

On either side
its ostrich neck
its camel neck
wavered,
swallowed the high
midnight.

The womb held back.
It had an eye
for sand,

spread its cool
oranges and reds
on dry land,

and bright
and fierce
as a lair,
the womb bear-hugged
its dead,
and let go.

if there are any heavens my mother will (all by
          herself) have
one. It will not be a pansy heaven nor
a fragile heaven of lilies-of-the-valley but
it will be a heaven of blackred roses

my father will be (deep like a rose
tall like a rose)

standing near my

(swaying over her
silent)
with eyes which are really petals and see

nothing with the face of a poet really which
is a flower and not a face with
hands
which whisper
This is my beloved my

                    (suddenly in sunlight

he will bow,

& the whole garden will bow)

CLEARANCES

in memoriam M.K.H., 1911–1984

She taught me what her uncle once taught her:
How easily the biggest coal block split
If you got the grain and hammer angled right.

The sound of that relaxed alluring blow,
Its co-opted and obliterated echo,
Taught me to hit, taught me to loosen,

Taught me between the hammer and the block
To face the music. Teach me now to listen,
To strike it rich behind the linear black.

I

A cobble thrown a hundred years ago
Keeps coming at me, the first stone
Aimed at a great-grandmother's turncoat brow.
The pony jerks and the riot's on.
She's crouched low in the trap
Running the gauntlet that first Sunday
Down the brae to Mass at a panicked gallop.
He whips on through the town to cries of "Lundy!"

Call her "The Convert". "The Exogamous Bride".
Anyhow, it is a genre piece
Inherited on my mother's side
And mine to dispose with now she's gone.
Instead of silver and Victorian lace,
The exonerating, exonerated stone.

II

Polished linoleum shone there. Brass taps shone.
The china cups were very white and big –
An unchipped set with sugar bowl and jug.
The kettle whistled. Sandwich and tea scone
Were present and correct. In case it run,
The butter must be kept out of the sun.
And don't be dropping crumbs. Don't tilt your chair.
Don't reach. Don't point. Don't make noise when
    you stir.

It is Number 5, New Row, Land of the Dead,
Where grandfather is rising from his place
With spectacles pushed back on a clean bald head
To welcome a bewildered homing daughter
Before she even knocks. "What's this? What's this?"
And they sit down in the shining room together.

III

When all the others were away at Mass
I was all hers as we peeled potatoes.
They broke the silence, let fall one by one
Like solder weeping off the soldering iron:
Cold comforts set between us, things to share
Gleaming in a bucket of clean water.
And again let fall. Little pleasant splashes
From each other's work would bring us to our senses.

So while the parish priest at her bedside
Went hammer and tongs at the prayers for the dying
And some were responding and some crying
I remembered her head bent towards my head,
Her breath in mine, our fluent dipping knives –
Never closer the whole rest of our lives.

IV

Fear of affectation made her affect
Inadequacy whenever it came to
Pronouncing words "beyond her". *Bertold Brek.*
She'd manage something hampered and askew
Every time, as if she might betray
The hampered and inadequate by too
Well-adjusted a vocabulary.
With more challenge than pride, she'd tell me, "You
Know all them things." So I governed my tongue
In front of her, a genuinely well-
Adjusted adequate betrayal
Of what I knew better. I'd *naw* and *aye*
And decently relapse into the wrong
Grammar which kept us allied and at bay.

V

The cool that came off sheets just off the line
Made me think the damp must still be in them
But when I took my corners of the linen
And pulled against her, first straight down the hem
And then diagonally, then flapped and shook
The fabric like a sail in a cross-wind,
They made a dried-out undulating thwack.
So we'd stretch and fold and end up hand to hand
For a split second as if nothing had happened
For nothing had that had not always happened
Beforehand, day by day, just touch and go,
Coming close again by holding back
In moves where I was X and she was O
Inscribed in sheets she'd sewn from ripped-out
    flour sacks.

VI

In the first flush of the Easter holidays
The ceremonies during Holy Week
Were highpoints of our *Sons and Lovers* phase.
The midnight fire. The paschal candlestick.
Elbow to elbow, glad to be kneeling next
To each other up there near the front
Of the packed church, we would follow the text
And rubrics for the blessing of the font.
As the hind longs for the streams, so my soul...
Dippings. Towellings. The water breathed on.
The water mixed with chrism and with oil.
Cruet tinkle. Formal incensation
And the psalmist's outcry taken up with pride:
Day and night my tears have been my bread.

VII

In the last minutes he said more to her
Almost than in all their life together.
"You'll be in New Row on Monday night
And I'll come up for you and you'll be glad
When I walk in the door ... Isn't that right?"
His head was bent down to her propped-up head.
She could not hear but we were overjoyed.
He called her good and girl. Then she was dead,
The searching for a pulsebeat was abandoned
And we all knew one thing by being there.
The space we stood around had been emptied
Into us to keep, it penetrated
Clearances that suddenly stood open.
High cries were felled and a pure change happened.

VIII

I thought of walking round and round a space
Utterly empty, utterly a source
Where the decked chestnut tree had lost its place
In our front hedge above the wallflowers.
The white chips jumped and jumped and skited high.
I heard the hatchet's differentiated
Accurate cut, the crack, the sigh
And collapse of what luxuriated
Through the shocked tips and wreckage of it all.
Deep-planted and long gone, my coeval
Chestnut from a jam jar in a hole,
Its heft and hush become a bright nowhere,
A soul ramifying and forever
Silent, beyond silence listened for.

INDEX OF AUTHORS

240

243

ACKNOWLEDGMENTS

Thanks are due to the following copyright holders for permission to reprint:

CHINUA ACHEBE: 'A Mother in a Refugee Camp' from *Christmas in Biafra and Other Poems* by Chinua Achebe, copyright © 1973 by Chinua Achebe. Used by permission of Doubleday, a division of Random House, Inc and David Higham Associates. FLEUR ADCOCK: 'On a Son Returned to New Zealand' from *Poems 1960–2000*, Bloodaxe Books, 2000. ANNA AKHMATOVA: 'Shards' from *The Complete Poems of Anna Akhmatova*, edited and translated by Judith Hemschemeyer, first published in 1993 in Great Britain by Canongate Books Ltd, 14 High St, Edinburgh EH1 1TE, and in the US and Canada by the Zephyr Press. YEHUDA AMICHAI: 'My Mother Once Told Me', translated by Assia Gutmann, Sheep Meadow Press. Hebrew-language version © 1994 by Yehuda Amichai. GEORGE BARKER: 'To My Mother' from *Collected Poems*, published by kind permission of Faber and Faber Ltd. ELIZABETH BISHOP: 'Sestina' from *The Complete Poems: 1927–1979* by Elizabeth Bishop, reprinted by kind permission of Farrar, Straus and Giroux LLC. Copyright © 1979, 1983 by Alice Helen Methfessel. EAVAN BOLAND: 'The Pomegranate,' 'The Blossom', 'The Black Lace My

248

right © 1991 by the Trustees for the E. E. Cummings Trust and George James Firmage. MAURA DOOLEY: 'Freight' from *Sound Barrier* by Maura Dooley (Bloodaxe Books, 2002) reprinted by kind permission of Bloodaxe Books. RITA DOVE: 'Genetic Expedition' reprinted by kind permission of W. W. Norton & Company, Inc. JANE DURAN: 'Miscarriages' reprinted by kind permission of Enitharmon Press. RUTH FAINLIGHT: 'Handbag' reprinted by kind permission of the author. ALLEN GINSBERG: 'Kaddish', excerpt as submitted from 'Kaddish' from *Collected Poems 1947–1980* by Allen Ginsberg. Copyright © 1959 by Allen Ginsberg. Reprinted by kind permission of HarperCollins Publishers Inc and the Penguin Group UK. NIKKI GIOVANNI: 'Legacies' from *My House* by Nikki Giovanni. Copyright © 1972 by Nikki Giovanni. Reprinted by kind permission of HarperCollins Publishers Inc. LOUISE GLÜCK: 'Illuminations' and 'Brown Circle' from *The First Four Books of Poems* by Louise Glück. Copyright © 1968, 1971, 1972, 1973, 1974, 1975, 1976, 1977, 1978, 1979, 1980, 1985, 1995 by Louise Glück. 'A Fable' from *Ararat* by Louise Glück. Copyright © 1990 by Louise Glück. Reprinted by kind permission of HarperCollins Publishers Inc. JORIE GRAHAM: 'Mother's Sewing Box' from *Hybrids of Plants and of Ghosts* © 1980 Princeton University Press. Reprinted by kind permission of Princeton University Press. EAMON GRENNAN: 'Heirloom' from

Although every effort has been made to trace and contact copyright holders, in a few instances this has not been possible. If notified, the publishers will be pleased to rectify any omission in future editions.